FORMULA ONE DRIVERS' PROFILES

SIMON SCOTT

Foulis

To my Mother and Father

ISBN 0 85429 312 4

First published 1982

© Simon Scott 1982

A FOULIS Motoring Book

Published by:
Haynes Publishing Group
Sparkford, Yeovil, Somerset BA22 7JJ,
England

Distributed in North America by:
Haynes Publications Inc.
861 Lawrence Drive, Newbury Park,
California 91320, USA

Editor: **Rod Grainger**
Cover design: **Joe Fitzgerald**
Cover photos & colour helmet designs:
Simon Scott
Printed in England by:
J.H. Haynes & Co. Ltd.

Contents

Foreword by Derek Daly

This superbly illustrated book covers the decade from 1971 to the present day. Not only are all the stars included, from Graham Hill and Jackie Stewart to Emerson Fittipaldi and Niki Lauda, but all the other points scorers as well – so even Lella Lombardi is featured in recognition of her sixth place in the accident shortened 1975 Spanish Grand Prix.

Perhaps it is this depth of coverage which attracted my interest most, as this book recounts the racing exploits of many who never really hit the limelight, yet without whom Grand Prix racing would be unable to survive... Another novel idea incorporated by the author is the colour helmet designs which will aid driver identification whilst spectating, not only at the track, but also via the television screen.

Simon Scott has written a book suitable for enthusiast and occasional spectator alike, and well worthy of any motor racing bookshelf!

Derek Daly

Acknowledgements

I would like to thank the many individuals and organisations whose co-operation has been so helpful, in particular Mike Kettlewell who helped me out of a number of tight corners. Special mention must also go to the following for their help and patience: Derek Daly, Howden Ganley, Graham Garrett, Rod Grainger, Alan Henry, Lady Hesketh, Lord Alexander Hesketh, Gordon Murray, Nelson Piquet, Philip Sandall and Marc Surer.

The author is also indebted to all those individuals and companies who supplied the photographs which add so much to this book. Photograph contributors are: Alfa Romeo, Beta Utensili, CSS Promotions/Saudia Leyland, Essex Motorsport, Ford Motor Co. Ltd., Guinness, LAT Photographic, Team Lotus International Ltd., Renault UK Ltd., Philip Sandall, Charles Stewart & Co. Ltd., Texaco, Tyrrell Racing Organisation Ltd., Unipart.

About the Author

Born and bred in the picturesque countryside near Northampton, the author seemed destined to come into contact with the motor racing fraternity at Silverstone. First introduced to this famous local track by a Life Member, the late Jack Frost, he quickly became enthusiastic – intoxicated with admiration for men and machines driven to their very limit. He had 'caught the bug' and soon was travelling, not only to Silverstone on a regular basis, but also to Brands Hatch and the Continental tracks.

Simon, the son of a Headmaster, was educated at Wellingborough School where he was Head of House and participated in a wide variety of sports, being selected for his School's Soccer and Rugby First teams.

From a participator to a spectator, Simon's first love has for many years been Grand Prix Motor Racing, and this book surely shows his dedication to the Sport.

Introduction

This book is intended as a miniature 'Who's Who' of every Formula 1 driver who has scored a single point, or more, in a World Championship Grand Prix since 1971. For each of these drivers, whether they have scored a single point, a win, or attained the ultimate accolade of becoming World Champion – there is a profile of their career, a photograph of them and their car, and a colour illustration of their helmet, together with a permanent record of their achievements in motor racing.

A real problem today, not only for spectators but for team managers and mechanics too, is that of driver recognition. This confusion is due to the similarity of each team's cars because of sponsors' liveries, the new computer-style lettering and the blurring effects of high speed.

In the Fifties it was possible to see not only the driver's face but his arms and shoulders as well, so it was easy to identify the likes of Ascari, Moss and Fangio, simply because each driver was so instantly recognisable by his well-known physical features. As the competitive world of Formula 1 made it necessary for car shapes to be more streamlined, the driver became more enclosed and hidden from the spectator's view than ever before. However, even in the early Sixties, there were still open-face helmets, making it possible, albeit with more difficulty, to recognise the faces of stars such as Jim Clark, Jack Brabham and Phil Hill. As full-faced helmets came into use during the Seventies, it became virtually impossible to recognise the stars through their helmet visors and protective clothing, unless one knew the colour of their eyes! The solution was simple – the plain helmets of the Fifties and Sixties gave way to brightly coloured individual designs which should provide instant recognition.

These modern helmet designs are like finger prints; although some may be similar in style none are actually duplicated. The reasons for particular designs are varied although the most popular choice is the colouring of the driver's national flag, as Nigel Mansell explained: '...being very patriotic and English – red, white and blue – what else?' Others have different reasons for their choice such as Emerson Fittipaldi who says of his helmet design 'I just like the colours!' Or as Jean-Pierre Jarier explains, 'Before I started racing I was a great fan of Jim Clark, whose helmet I mistakenly thought was green, so, naturally, I wanted a green helmet too, but I added white to give a distinctive design.' Ironically, Niki Lauda's original 'day-glow' red helmet was dreamt up by the Austrian as a safety measure, just in case he should be thrown out of his car, in his earlier days of racing round the Nurburgring – the site of his near-fatal accident in 1976. However, for his comeback drive in the 1982 South African Grand Prix Niki used a helmet with his airline's motif on the side. His great rival James Hunt, meanwhile, based his design on the colours of his Old School – Wellington College. The superstitious Irishman, Derek Daly says, 'My helmet design represents my birth sign, Pisces' and the enthusiastic Graham Hill loyally chose the colours of his London Rowing Club.

Simon Scott

This Italian racing driver was born on October 3, 1941 of wealthy parents. It was while he was studying for a law degree that he became interested in racing; starting with hillclimbing in 1962. He raced Formula 3 for a time, but really made his name in saloon car racing, his first major victory being in the 1965 Monza 4-hours before winning the European Touring Car Championship the following year in a works Alfa Romeo GTA.

Having won the 1967 Tourist Trophy, Andrea was signed by Ferrari who liked the idea of an Italian in their Formula 1 team. His F1 debut came in South Africa but Andrea injured his neck during practice for the Race of Champions, effectively putting him out of racing until the end of the year when he returned to win the Argentinian Temporada Championship in a Formula 2 Ferrari.

In 1969, during a lean patch in his career, Andrea drove a Formula 5000 Surtees before moving back to Formula 1 in 1970 after persuading Alfa Romeo to let him have one of their engines to put into a McLaren M7D – unfortunately this venture brought little success. Despite another miserable Formula 1 season in 1971, this time with a March 711-Alfa Romeo, Andrea ended Alfa Romeo's

Andrea de Adamich.

twenty years without a major international race success by winning both the Brands Hatch and Watkins Glen rounds in the Sports Car Championship.

In 1972, despite battling on without credit in the Surtees team, Andrea surprised many in Spain when he drove

Andrea scored an encouraging 4th place in the 1972 Spanish Grand Prix with his Surtees TS9B.

the Formula 1 race of his life, fighting off Revson and Pace to take 4th place. Encouraging drives came in the non-Championship races of Vallelunga and Brands Hatch with a 2nd and a 3rd place respectively.

After one more race in the Surtees in 1973, Andrea drove a Brabham, coming 4th in Belgium in only his second drive for the team. However, at Silverstone, in the infamous multi-car accident at the beginning of lap 2, Andrea was trapped in his car for nearly an hour before he could be taken to hospital for treatment of his leg injuries.

This accident put the Italian out of Formula 1. After recovering from his injuries and another year of racing Alfa Romeo Sports cars he retired.

For the Record

First GP
1968 Africa (Ferrari 312)

Best GP result
4th 1972 Spain (Surtees TS9B)
4th 1973 Belgium (Brabham BT37)

Chris was born in Bulls on the North Island of New Zealand on July 20, 1943, the son of a sheep farmer. At 17 he raced an Austin A40 and other cars in various races before being brought to Europe by Reg Parnell to compete in his first Formula 1 race at Goodwood on Easter Monday 1963 at the age of 19. Young Chris had a promising race debut in the Belgian Grand Prix and stayed with the Parnell team in 1964 to become the second youngest driver ever to score a World Championship point when he came 5th in the Dutch Grand Prix driving a Lotus 25-BRM.

Despite competing in only three GPs in the years 1965-66 Chris won his first major race in 1966 – Le Mans, co-driving with Bruce McLaren. Ferrari signed up Chris and he stayed with them for the next three years having the most successful season of his career in 1967, when he notched up four 3rd places to finish 4th in the World Championship. It was during this year that he gained the 'unlucky' tag, for he had to retire in France, when he lay 2nd, and in the United States when he was about to take the lead. Compensation came with two Sportscar wins at Daytona and Monza!

Another instance of his bad luck occurred in the 1968 Spanish Grand Prix when Chris had built up a 25-second lead over Hill only to have a fuse blow in the fuel pump, forcing retirement! His superb performance in practice did produce one 2nd at the British Grand Prix, even though he seldom seemed to keep up his qualifying pace during the ensuing race.

After winning the Formula 2 Tasman Championship in a Ferrari Dino early in 1969 many expected this to be a successful year for him in Formula 1. Full of natural talent, Chris dominated the Spanish Grand Prix building up a 25 second lead over Stewart until the inevitable happened – this time the retirement was due to engine failure....

Moving to the new March team in 1970, Chris proceeded to score his first Formula 1 win at Silverstone – the only problem being that it was the non-Championship International Trophy

Chris Amon.

meeting! At Monaco misfortune continued for, after holding 2nd place for 60 laps of the 80 lap race, his suspension broke after a gallant run. Second places followed in Belgium and France.

In a Matra-Simca for 1971, Chris scored the second Formula 1 win of his career in the non-Championship Argentine GP, and looked like repeating the performance in Italy as he'd set pole position. Once again Chris led until, dogged by bad luck, he adjusted his helmet and in the process lost his complete visor. This, combined with fuel starvation problems on the last lap, dropped the New Zealander down to 6th place.

Bad luck again struck in 1972. In the Belgian GP he was heading for 3rd place when he ran out of fuel and in the French GP was on pole by nearly a second, led the race convincingly, set fastest lap and then picked up a puncture! Rejoining the race in 8th place he pulled up to an incredible 3rd by the finish. At Le Mans it was a similar story, for Chris's car retired seconds after moving into the lead!

After failing to secure a place in the

Chris was at his most inspired during the 1972 French Grand Prix, for, although a puncture delayed his impressive drive in a Matra, he set fastest lap to pull up to 3rd by the finish.

March team for the 1973 season, Chris found himself without a regular Formula 1 drive. Instead he drove a Tecno to 6th place in Belgium, and a Tyrrell in Canada.

Disillusioned with uncompetitive machinery, Chris had even built his own car, but the Amon AF1 raced only once, in Spain 1974. After racing on and off with BRM and Ensign, Chris had a fuller season with the Ensign team in 1976, surprising many with his speed in the outdated car, especially in Sweden, where he qualified an amazing 3rd! Changing to Williams later in the year Chris spun in practice for the Canadian GP and was hit by Ertl, resulting in pulled tendons in his left knee. Recovered, Chris started 1977 racing a Can-Am Wolf Dallara but soon announced his retirement and concentrated on managing the team for the test of the year.

Chris is now a fulltime dairy-farmer in his home town of Bulls, and owns a 1,200 acre farm.

With better luck Chris could have retired with half-a-dozen Grand Prix wins to his credit, but it seems that Chris was destined never to win a Grand Prix, although he did score two non-Championship Formula 1 wins. Chris was a talented driver, constantly dogged by bad luck, a driver considered by Enzo Ferrari as the best test driver he ever had, and that included Lauda!

For The Record

First GP
1963 Belgium (Lola-Climax)

Best GP result
2nd 1968 Britain (Ferrari 312)
2nd 1970 Belgium (March 701)
2nd 1970 France (March 701)

One of the world's most versatile drivers, Mario was born in Italy on February 28, 1940. Whilst still a teenager he emigrated with his family to America, having already been enthralled by watching his hero Ascari at the Italian Grand Prix. Once in America, he began racing modified stock cars in the late 1950s and, in 1961, he started a successful career in midget racing. Upon gaining his USAC licence in 1964, he immediately proved dominant, winning the Championship in 1965, 1966 and 1969 and finishing as runner-up in 1967 and 1968. Having won the 1967 NASCAR Daytona 500 and the 1969 Indianapolis 500, Mario thought seriously of racing in Formula 1, although he would only be able to race occasionally because of his USAC commitments.

His first foray came with Lotus in 1968, and, amazingly, he started his first Grand Prix at Watkins Glen from pole position! After a further limited season with Lotus, in 1969, and with March in 1970, Mario raced occasionally for Ferrari in 1971, winning first time out for the team in South Africa after a tremendous drive which credited him with fastest lap. Successful in Ferrari sports cars as well, his loose arrangement with the team continued until 1972.

The 'lure of the dollar' kept Mario in the States until 1975 when he practically

Mario Andretti.

competed in a full season of Grand Prix racing with Parnelli. The project proved unsuccessful, but Mario found compensation when he finished 2nd in the United States Formula 5000 Championship. With Parnelli abandoning Formula 1 early in 1976, Andretti joined Team Lotus when they were at a low point in their history with the type 77 proving to be a midfield

Mario driving an Alfa Romeo during 1981 with which he had hoped to recapture the success he had gained with Lotus in 1978.

runner. However, Mario as team leader soon came to grips with the car to lead the Swedish Grand Prix before his engine blew – completing the year with a fine win in Japan, having lapped the entire field in the process!

In 1977, Mario's practice form (which included no less than seven pole positions!) should have resulted in his becoming World Champion. However, in the races he was so often let down by engine failures that four wins – at Long Beach, Jarama, Dijon and Monza – were simply not enough to wrest the title from the consistent Lauda.

A conclusive win with the old Lotus 78 in Argentina gave a foretaste of things to come in 1978. When the Lotus 79 was first raced, in Belgium, Mario achieved a fine start-to-finish victory and led no less than eight of the next nine races, winning in Spain, France, Germany and Holland, to take the World Championship!

Practically unbeatable in 1978, 1979 was vastly different for Mario. The revolutionary new Lotus 80 failed to fulfil its promise to become a world-beater, although Mario managed to score a 3rd with it in Spain. If 1979 was below expectations, 1980 proved to be even worse. Despite good runs in Argentina, Holland, Monaco and Britain, Mario only scored one point and that was for 6th place in the year's final race at Watkins Glen.

In an attempt to find a competitive car, Mario joined Alfa Romeo for 1981, but an encouraging 4th on his debut for the team at Long Beach proved to be his best result of the year. Disillusioned with the vicissitudes of fate in Formula 1, Mario finally decided to take the heart-breaking step of retiring from Grand Prix racing at the end of the year.

Mario had shown his undoubted brilliance in 1978, when he won the World Championship, but after that he floundered with machinery unworthy of his talent. He has not, however, retired altogether from motor racing as he has a full season of competition on America's oval tracks lined up for 1982 with 'Patrick Racing'.

For The Record

First GP
1968 United States (Lotus 49)

GP Wins
1971 South Africa (Ferrari 312B)
1976 Japan (Lotus 77)
1977 United States, West (Lotus 78)
1977 Spain (Lotus 78)
1977 France (Lotus 78)
1977 Italy (Lotus 78)
1978 Argentina (Lotus 78)
1978 Belgium (Lotus 79)
1978 Spain (Lotus 79)
1978 France (Lotus 79)
1978 Germany (Lotus 79)
1978 Holland (Lotus 79)

World Champion
1978 (Lotus)

This wealthy Italian playboy was born on March 26, 1958, the son of a construction company boss and powerboat enthusiast. His first taste of speed came when he partnered his father in powerboats but, in 1972, Elio turned to Karting, becoming a member of the Italian National Team.

1974 saw Elio win the Italian Championship. Runner-up in the 1976 Kart World Championship, Elio followed some unsuccessful Formula Italia outings with a Formula 3 season in 1977. After scintillating performances at Monaco and Monza he had his first taste of Formula 2 before the year's end – leading at Misano! Although showing flair and potential in Formula 2, Elio's best result of 1978 came when he relegated himself to Formula 3 for the prestigious Monaco event, and won! Having aroused interest from Formula 1 teams, the young Italian joined Shadow in 1979. Although the car was not really competitive, Elio never gave up trying and gained useful Grand Prix experience culminating with a fine 4th place at Watkins Glen.

Impressing Lotus during a test session, he was signed up to drive alongside Andretti in 1980. Well up the grids in South America, Elio finished a faultless, mature 2nd in Brazil after a determined drive from 7th on the grid. His incredible fire and enthusiasm were rewarded by points in Austria and Italy, finishing off the 1980 season in excellent

Elio de Angelis.

form with a 4th in the States.

1981 boded well for Elio, whose natural talent was rewarded with the enviable position of team leader at Lotus. Indeed, the season started well with a 3rd in South Africa, but the Lotus 88 controversy prevented serious development of the existing chassis. The result was a 4th, in Italy, along with four 5th places and three 6ths. Elio will, no doubt, be hoping for greater success during 1982....

For The Record

First GP
1979 Argentina (Shadow DN9B)

Best GP Result
2nd 1980 Brazil (Lotus 81)

Elio at Long Beach in the Lotus 81 which had helped him to an incredible 2nd place in the Brazilian Grand Prix earlier in 1980.

This diminutive, and quietly spoken Frenchman was born on July 4, 1948, the son of a motor racing enthusiast. Like so many of today's Grand Prix drivers Rene's career began in karting, becoming a member of the French national kart team before his military service.

In 1970 he went to Italy to work as a mechanic for Conrero. Rene's string of motor racing successes began when he won the Formula Renault series in 1973. From there he moved to Formula 5000, but with little luck, so he raced in Formula Renault Europe in 1975, winning the Championship.

For the 1976 season Rene took the obvious stepping-stone – to European Formula 2. He won three races out of the twelve in the series in the Martini Renault and came 2nd in the championship – one point behind Jabouille! Rene made sure of the title in 1977, winning at Silverstone, Pau and Nogaro in the Martini Renault Mk 22 and the following year he had a limited, unsuccessful, Formula 1 season with the Martini Mk 23 project.

Rene's big break came when Renault signed him up for the 1979 season. At first the Renault proved unreliable and Rene seemed inexperienced, but the appearance of a

Rene Arnoux.

new turbo-charging unit at the French GP immediately put him on the front row of the grid. He finished 3rd after having an amazing wheel-to-wheel battle with Villeneuve in the last two laps. A 2nd position in the British Grand Prix was followed by his first pole position, in Austria, but his 2nd place in the race was lost when he ran out of fuel near the finish. Pole position in Holland was also wasted, this time by a startline collision,

Bad luck dogged Rene during 1981. Here, in the British Grand Prix, driving a Renault Turbo, he led for most of the race – having qualified on pole position – only to retire a handful of laps from the end.

but the season ended with a fine 2nd place at Watkins Glen.

The 1980 season started well for Rene. He won both the Brazilian and South African Grand Prix to put him at the top of the World Championship points table. This lead was short-lived however, and, although Rene secured three pole positions on the trot near the end of the season, his best result was only a 2nd place in Holland.

In 1981, mechanical unreliability meant that Rene's practice successes (four pole positions) were not followed by race victories, although consolation came in the form of a 2nd in Austria. Surely, when the Renault's reliability matches its speed, Rene will be a strong contender for the World Championship?

For The Record

First GP
1978 Belgium (Martini Mk. 23)

GP Wins
1980 Brazil (Renault RE21)
1980 South Africa (Renault RE21)

The son of a butcher, Jean-Pierre was born in Paris on April 6, 1937, and started his racing career on motorcycles, winning no less than eleven National Championships! Becoming a mechanic at the Bonnet works, Jean-Pierre secured a drive with them, winning his class in the 1963 Le Mans.

Moving up to Formula 2 and GTs in 1964, Jean-Pierre was lucky to survive a fiery crash at the Rheims 12-hours – an accident that has left him with a limp and a weak left arm to this day. Undeterred, after a six month recovery he returned to the cockpit in 1965 to win the French Formula 3 Championship.

In 1966 Jean-Pierre won the Monaco Formula 3 race, as well as competing for Matra in Formula 2. The following year he entered the Grand Prix scene in a Formula 2 Matra ballasted to meet the minimum Formula 1 weight limit. So when he made his debut at Watkins Glen he was technically driving a Formula 1 car, despite only having a 1600cc engine – nevertheless he finished a creditable 7th!

Into F1 Grand Prix fulltime with Matra in 1968, Jean-Pierre soon made his mark by leading the Spanish event, before being forced to pit, and by finishing 2nd in Holland, despite a spin and a pit stop – setting fastest lap on

Jean-Pierre Beltoise.

both occasions. Hailed as a new French hero, he capped his year by winning the European Formula 2 Championship.

With Tyrrell in 1969, his ability was rewarded by 3rd places in Spain and Italy, and a superb 2nd, behind team leader Stewart, in France where he overtook Ickx on the very last lap! Inspired in front of his home crowd at

In the wet at Monaco in 1972, Jean-Pierre was unbeatable in his BRM – leading from start to finish to score the only Grand Prix victory of his career.

Clermont-Ferrand in 1970, Jean-Pierre pressurised and eventually passed Ickx to take the lead: only to sustain a puncture and fuel problems....

Although further excellent drives in Austria and Italy followed in 1970, it was not until he joined, and led, the BRM team in 1972 that he proved victorious. The setting was a very wet Monaco, where from 4th on the grid Jean-Pierre swept into an immediate lead. He was never passed in this race and set fastest lap on his way to a total domination of the event, a result of his superb car control.

A further Formula 1 victory followed at a non-Championship Brands Hatch race but, unfortunately, although he came very close in the wet 1973 Canadian event, he was never to win a Grand Prix again. The highlight of his last Formula 1 season in 1974 with BRM was a sensational 2nd in South Africa where he set fastest lap during an aggressive drive.

However, as Jean-Pierre's Formula 1 career ended, his Sports Car career blossomed. He won four endurance races during 1974 and, although he nearly landed the Ligier Grand Prix drive at the beginning of 1976, his international racing career concluded with a series of outings at Le Mans. Today he is still one of the leading figures in the French Group 1 Saloon Car Championship.

At his best, Jean-Pierre was brilliant, as was shown by his dominant display at Monaco in 1972, a race that gave this gifted Frenchman his only Grand Prix victory.

For The Record

First GP
1967 United States (Matra MS7)
GP Win
1972 Monaco (BRM P160B)

Tommy 'Slim' Borgudd was born on November 25, 1946, and began racing in 1970, winning sixteen Formula Ford races the following year. In 1972 he was Swedish 2-litre Sports Car Champion and in 1973 he won the Swedish Formula Ford series.

After this success, Slim ran out of money and had to revert to his former profession, that of drummer. It was not until 1978 that Slim took up racing again, competing in the European Formula 3 championship. In 1979, despite a low budget and working as his own mechanic, Slim finished 3rd in the series, his results including a fine 2nd place at Flugplatz Kassel-Calden. In 1980, Slim planned a full season in Formula 2, but sponsorship fell through, so instead he competed occasionally in Formula 3.

With the backing of his long-time friends in the 'Abba' pop group, Slim entered the world of Grand Prix racing in 1981 at San Marino with ATS. To everyone's surprise, the talented Swede managed to qualify despite his lack of experience and a less-than-competitive car. However, it was not until the British Grand Prix that Slim qualified again. Benefitting from the high retirement rate, Slim finished 6th in what was effectively his second Grand Prix, and regularly qualified for the rest of the season. His potential now established, Slim has

Slim Borgudd.

signed a three-year contract with Tyrrell, which is likely to bring further success.

For The Record

First GP
1981 San Marino (ATS D4)

Best GP Result
6th 1981 Britain (ATS HGS1)

Benefitting from a high retirement rate in the 1981 British Grand Prix, Slim scored a 6th place in his ATS.

Vittorio the wild, likeable Italian, was born on November 11, 1937, at Monza. A partner in a family garage business near the famous local track, Vittorio began motorcycle racing in 1957. The next year he was Italian 175cc Motorcycle Champion and began to mix both two-wheel and four-wheel activities – winning the 1961 200cc World Kart Championship.

After working for his elder brother, Tino, as a mechanic, Vittorio decided to become a competitor again in 1968. His suicidal overtaking manoeuvres at this stage in his career earned him the nickname of "The Monza Gorilla". Still unknown outside Italy, Vittorio surprised the Formula 2 world in 1970 when he came 2nd at the Salzburgring, beating the likes of Quester, Fittipaldi and Hill! Having won, between spins, the Italian Formula 2 title in 1972, Vittorio moved on to tackle the European Championship in 1973.

After a steady start to the season, Vittorio won at the Salzburgring and at Albi, to finish 2nd in the overall placings. His sponsors, Beta Tools, bought his way into the March Formula 1 team in 1974 – Vittorio making his debut in South Africa. In Sweden he fought his way up to 5th before his engine blew on the last lap and in Austria he scored his first World Championship point.

With the arrival of the new, simple, neat and light March 751 early in the 1975 season, the Italian found himself becoming a front runner – indeed, in Belgium he was leading by lap 5 having passed both Lauda and Pace, but slipped back to 3rd before retiring. In Sweden Vittorio dominated practice to set pole position and led the race from the start until he had to pit for a fresh tyre. Poor consolation came in the way of 6th place in Britain, but in Austria Vittorio pulled off a surprise win in the wet, a truly tremendous display of driving on the edge of disaster in terrible conditions – passing both Lauda and Hunt and settling fastest lap. On his 'cooling down' lap Vittorio added to his reputation by spinning and crunching the nose of his March. He gained only half points for his

Vittorio Brambilla.

victory as the race was shortened due to bad weather. In Formula 2, Vittorio won at Vallelunga and in typical fashion triggered off an accident which eliminated two major Championship contenders in Sicily.

1976 saw Vittorio back to his old tricks of testing circuit catchfencing and guardrails. He nevertheless shone at various stages in the season, but only picked up a point in Holland.

In seventeen starts during 1977, Vittorio silenced critics by finishing in twelve of the races: a record beaten only by the Ferrari drivers. In Belgium he managed to push his Surtees into the lead, finishing 4th. Far more successful than his team-mates, he came 5th in Germany and finished the year with a fine drive in Canada – fighting with Depailler for 3rd place (which would have become 2nd place on Andretti's retirement) before shooting off the oily road, two laps from the end, to be classified 6th. Success also came in the Alfa Romeo T33SC sports car with four wins.

A poor 1978 season with Surtees yielded only a 6th place in Austria. In Italy, Vittorio was lucky to survive the

Vittorio at the wheel of the March 751 with which he won the rain-shortened 1975 Austrian Grand Prix.

massive start-line accident in which Ronnie Peterson died. Vittorio sustained head injuries and was, for a time, in a critical condition; however, he made a slow recovery and eventually returned to drive an Alfa Romeo at the 1979 Italian and Canadian Grands Prix.

After another year's lay-off, Vittorio raced in Holland in 1980 but his performance was ragged and he retired after the Italian Grand Prix. Vittorio was a good competitor who loved the sport – driving his cars on, or more usually over, the limit. One of Formula One's characters who led a charmed life!

For The Record

First GP
1974 South Africa (March 741)

GP win
1975 Austria (March 751)

Born on March 25, 1952, Tony was the eldest son of the three-times World Stock Car Champion, Johnny Brise. After initial success in karting, Tony started motor racing at 18 and, by the time he had graduated with an honours degree in business administration, he had swept the board in about 25 Formula Ford races.

In 1972 Tony moved up into Formula 3, and in 1973 seemed almost unbeatable, winning the John Player title from Alan Jones, winning the Lombard North Central title and coming 2nd in the Forward Trust Championship.

Three victories in 1974, taking Tony to 3rd place in the John Player Formula 2 Atlantic Championship, proved to be the backdrop to six successive wins in 1975, which gave him the title. When Williams offered him a Formula One drive in the Spanish GP Tony accepted and finished an encouraging 7th. This drive led to Graham Hill signing up the young Briton to race his car. In his first race in the 'Hill' Tony qualified 7th, fractionally quicker than World Champion Fittipaldi! In the next race Tony scored his first World Championship point with a 6th place in Sweden, after gear trouble had dropped him from 5th! Despite a number of crashes in the last few races of the 1975 season much was expected from Tony in 1976, but then disaster struck....

Returning home from testing at Paul Ricard on the foggy night of November

Tony Brise.

29, 1975, fate decreed that Tony should be in Graham Hill's plane when it crashed. The motor racing world was saddened to hear that these two fine drivers, and four other team members, were killed. Tony Brise, probably the greatest prospect for British motor racing was dead.

For The Record

First GP
1975 Spain (Williams FW03)

Best GP result
6th 1975 Sweden (Embassy-Hill GH)

Tony scored the only Championship point of his tragically shortened career in the 1975 Swedish Grand Prix driving a Hill.

Andrea's first rise from karts to Formula 1 was extremely fast, perhaps too fast for the fiery young Italian, who was born on May 31, 1959. He has lived in Rome all his life and started racing in karts, winning a number of National and International Championships, before graduating to cars at the end of 1977. In his three Super Ford races he won two and finished 2nd in the other. With the backing of Marlboro, Andrea competed in the British Formula 3 Championships in 1978 and 1979. Almost immediately he proved to be a front runner, although it took him a year to score his first victory.

During 1979, Andrea won six races in the Formula 3 series, showing himself to be one of the quickest drivers on his day, to finish 2nd in the Championship behind Chico Serra. Moving on to Formula 2 in 1980, Andrea won at Misano and was quickly offered an Alfa Romeo Formula 1 drive at the end of the season.

Making his Grand Prix debut in

Andrea de Cesaris.

Canada, Andrea ran 7th before retirement, having qualified well. Another good showing in the States prompted McLaren to sign up the aggressive, but erratic, Italian for 1981. Struggling with an outdated car, Andrea

Andrea in the McLaren MP4 which he raced from the 1981 Monaco Grand Prix until the end of the season.

did well to finish 6th at San Marino. The arrival of the new McLaren MP4 immediately allowed Andrea to qualify high on the grid, although he soon gained the reputation of being a crasher. This was not entirely Andrea's fault for, although he made many silly mistakes, other accidents were the result of errors by more established drivers. Anyway, Andrea's confidence seemed to wane and he gradually slipped down the grid in qualifying.

Andrea hopes to re-establish his undoubted ability by rejoining Alfa Romeo in 1982.

For The Record

First GP
1980 Canada (Alfa Romeo 179)

Best GP Result
6th 1981 San Marino (McLaren M29C)

Born on February 25, 1944, this handsome Parisian won his first car in a Shell Scholarship scheme in 1967. Known, in his early days, as 'Beltoise's brother-in-law' Francois soon made a name for himself by winning the 1968 French Formula 3 Championship. 1969 saw Francois in a Formula 2 Tecno, but only at Rheims did he really shine, although he competed in the Formula 2 division of the German Grand Prix.

Despite continuing in Formula 2 with Tecno in 1970, Francois' big break came when he was asked to replace Servoz-Gavin in Ken Tyrrell's March at the Dutch Grand Prix. After sensible drives, the young Frenchman scored his first World Championship point in Italy and looked set to take three more in Canada until he was forced to pit with a broken shock absorber while in 4th position.

1971 proved Francois to be a very worthy team-mate to a champion for, in France and Germany, he ably backed up Jackie Stewart on his way to victory. In Austria he retired when 2nd and in Italy, two weeks later, he finished 3rd, a mere 0.09 seconds behind the winner! He demonstrated his outstanding talent in the United States, where he overtook

Francois Cevert.

Stewart's ailing car on his way to a fine win. In Formula 2 he dominated the early season races, winning at Hockenheim and the Nurburgring, but failed to score after that, yet finished 5th overall in the Championship.

Disappointing in 1972, having finished 3rd in the F1 Championship the

Francois at speed during the 1973 Brazilian Grand Prix before his Tyrrell picked up a puncture (while lying 6th) from broken glass on the track. Despite this setback he finished in the points in eight consecutive races later in the season.

year before, Francois nevertheless scored two second places – in Belgium and the United States – and a fourth in France to take 6th place in the Championship. Showing his versatility he also finished 2nd at Le Mans in a Matra-Simca shared with Ganley.

1973 promised much, following a brilliant drive in Argentina during which Francois led for much of the race only to be overtaken by Emerson Fittipaldi eleven laps from the finish. A series of no less than eight successive finishes in the points started in Spain, where, having outqualified Stewart, he finished 2nd despite a pit stop which had dropped him to 13th! In Belgium he looked a sure winner, until brake failure forced him to make a deliberate spin – but even though this lost him seven places, a stirring drive, including a fastest lap, gave the determined Francois 2nd place. A steady drive in front of his home crowd was rewarded by another 2nd, while in Holland and Germany he backed up Stewart to finish 2nd again in the Tyrrell

dominated races, moving him up to 2nd in the World Championship points table. Tragically, a 5th in Italy was the impressive Frenchman's last finish in the points, for, at Watkins Glen – the scene of jubilation two years earlier – he crashed during practice with fatal consequences.

France had lost one of her finest drivers, a man who refused to be overshadowed by his team leader Stewart, a man who was a dominant force in endurance racing for Matra, and a man who was above all an excellent Formula 1 driver. The record shows only one win, but don't forget the ten 2nd places....

For The Record

First GP
1970 Holland (March 701)

GP Win
1971 United States (Tyrrell 002)

Born on January 10, 1957, this Arizona born vegetarian has lived most of his life in Rome. Four years in karts, culminating in a European Championship while still a teenager, led Eddie to turn to Formula Ford to make his motor racing debut in 1975.

Swiftly moving up to Formula 3, he took the "circus" by storm when he won his second Formula 3 race by passing Ribero on the outside of Woodcote at Silverstone. He won there again a week later but after1 that his results deteriorated. 1976 saw the young American compete in his first season of Formula 2 with some erratic drives, although finishing a fine 3rd at Enna.

1977 saw Eddie finish as runner-up to Arnoux in the European Formula 2 Championship. Although occasionally lacking maturity, his performances at Rouen and the Nurburgring were remarkable. Indeed, Ferrari were so impressed that they allowed him to test their Formula 1 car.

The new Theodore Formula 1 outfit offered Eddie a chance to gain his first real Formula 1 experience, although failing to qualify the uncompetitive car in South America. He made his Grand Prix debut in South Africa with a Hesketh before returning to Formula 2 for the

Eddie Cheever.

remainder of the season. A seasoned Formula 2 campaigner, Eddie won three races for the Osella team in 1979 and stayed with them when the team graduated to Formula 1 in 1980. Gradually, Eddie hauled the overweight, unreliable car onto the grids – running 3rd in Spain before retiring.

Joining the experienced Tyrrell team in 1981, Eddie scored his first World Championship points for a 5th place at Long Beach. A lucky 6th and a

The Tyrrell 011 first appeared during practice for the 1981 British Grand Prix, and although Eddie wrote off the chassis before the race he went on to finish 4th in his old car.

determined 5th in Belgium and Monaco respectively were followed by a 4th in Britain which nearly became 3rd when Laffite slowed on the last lap! The debut of a new Tyrrell came in Germany where it gained a 5th, but thereafter failed to finish. Eleventh place in the 1981 World Championship, combined with his confident, taut attitude on the track and a technical approach to the car, has led Talbot-Ligier to sign up the budding American star for 1982. This will be his most competitive drive yet, but will he now take Formula 1 by storm as he has Formula 3 and Formula 2?

For The Record

First GP
1978 South Africa (Hesketh 308E)

Best GP Result
4th 1981 Britain (Tyrrell 010)

A friendly Irishman, born in Dublin on March 11, 1953, Derek began his career in 1970 racing stock cars at Santry Stadium. Having won the Irish Stock Car Racing Championship in 1972, and finished runner-up in 1973, Derek started to race seriously in 1974.

Soon a winner in Formula Ford, he also won a hillclimb championship. Racing on a £1000 bank loan in 1974, by the end of the year his finances were in such a bad way that he and a friend went to Australia to work in the mines – returning with £2000 each! With this money Derek bought a new Formula Ford car. Time and again Derek led races, but something always seemed to go wrong. However, when he wrote-off the car, Crossle impressed by his talent, gave him a new one! Derek set pole position for the remaining nine races, winning eight on the trot to clinch the 1975 Irish Formula Ford Championship.

Arriving in England, Derek immediately made his mark by setting fastest lap at the Snetterton Formula Ford Festival. On Derek's own admission, '1976 was the hardest year of my life ... living in a converted 56-seater coach.' Even so, he won 23 races, including the Festival. Showing ever-increasing maturity to add to his undoubted speed, Derek moved up to Formula 3 in 1977. He made a great impression by beating Piquet in Austria, and won the BP Formula 3 title by winning the final four races of the series. His promise was proven when he made his impressive Formula 2 debut at Estoril, finishing 5th and setting fastest lap.

This remarkable young driver was soon wanted in Formula 1. Despite having tested a Theodore in December 1977, Derek joined the Hesketh F1 team to drive in the Silverstone International Trophy. Incredibly, he led, albeit for a matter of seconds, in appalling conditions before spinning when his helmet visor broke. However, his attempts to qualify the car for the Monaco and Belgian Grands Prix failed, but given an Ensign for the British Grand Prix, Derek qualified easily and was

Derek Daly.

running 8th until he lost a wheel, to end a very fine drive. His next race in Austria saw Derek run 4th, in the wet, for a time before spinning. Finally, he scored a point in Canada for 6th place, having diced with Pironi for the entire race. Derek also picked up two surprise Formula 2 wins in Italy, to finish 3rd in the Championship.

After a disappointing start in 1979, Derek left Ensign mid-season to concentrate on Formula 2. With a win at Donington he finished 3rd in the Championship, five points behind the winner. A remarkable feat considering he only competed in eight of the twelve rounds.

Jarier's hepatitis attack allowed Derek to take his place with Tyrrell for the F1 Austrian Grand Prix. He was also offered a further two drives in North America, running 3rd at the Glen before spinning off.

A full-time driver for Tyrrell in 1980, Derek settled down well to score a 4th in Argentina. Although he did make the

But for a pit stop early in the 1981 British Grand Prix, Derek would have finished an incredible 3rd – instead he finished 7th in his March 811.

occasional mistake, a horrifying series of accidents throughout most of the season were not a reflection on the talent of the Irishman who was on fine form when he scored a 4th in Britain.

Despite joining March as Number 1 driver in 1981, it was not until the team concentrated on one car, from Spain onwards, that Derek was able to qualify. Brilliant drives at Silverstone, after an early pitstop, and at Montreal followed. A man for the future, Derek is determined and fast, and now only needs a good car

to prove he can win races. Joining Theodore for 1982 may provide the opportunity he needs.

For The Record

First GP
1978 Britain (Ensign N177)

Best GP Result
4th 1980 Argentina (Tyrrell 009)
4th 1980 Britain (Tyrrell 010)

Born on August 9, 1944, the son of an architect, Patrick started his career on two wheels, but moved on to racing Lotus 7s in 1966. A long spell at Alpine Renault led to success in both Formula 3 and Sports Cars, culminating in Patrick's winning the 1971 French Formula 3 Championship.

In 1972, the determined Frenchman moved up into Formula 2 with March, finishing 3rd in the Championship. In winning the prestigious Monaco Formula 3 race, Patrick attracted the attention of Ken Tyrrell who gave him drives in France and America later in the year. Four 2nd places in Formula 2 during 1973 were enough for Tyrrell to sign up Patrick for the next season. However, during the winter, Patrick broke his leg motorcycling and had to race in Argentina in great pain — but, nevertheless, came 6th!

The advent of the new Tyrrell 007 later in 1974 brought a new competitiveness to the team, with Patrick taking his first, and only, pole position of his career in Sweden. In the race he finished 2nd, setting fastest lap, behind team-mate Scheckter. Compensation came in Formula 2 where Patrick won four races and the title in his March BMW 742.

After a disappointing 1975 season it

Patrick Depailler.

was Patrick who did much of the testing for the revolutionary Tyrrell P34 in 1976 but even so he seemed to be doomed not to win a race; he came 2nd no fewer than five times! Towards the end of the year his bad luck seemed to increase, for, in Canada, he pressured Hunt for practically the whole race before dropping back. When he crossed the line Patrick stopped and slumped, semi-conscious, in the cockpit — for the last eighteen laps he'd had fuel leaking into his cockpit which had made him drowsy — only the pain from his fuel-soaked overalls keeping him awake!

Patrick in the promising Alfa Romeo in which, sadly, he lost his life whilst testing at Hockenheim on July 1, 1980.

Modifications to the six-wheeler made excess weight and tyre problems combine to produce only moderate results in 1977. So for 1978 Tyrrell produced a four-wheeled car which, although reliable, was never really totally competitive. Patrick made the most of his machinery though, and in South Africa seemed certain to take his first win as he was leading the race, but unhappily the lead was lost on the last lap to Peterson when Patrick ran out of fuel! Monaco was different, for Patrick ran 2nd from the start, driving an inspired race, and taking the lead when Watson retired. Although this win put him in the lead of the World Championship, mid-season mechanical failures spoilt any title hope.

Joining Ligier for 1979 Patrick showed himself as a possible World Champion by winning in Spain. Unfortunately a hang-gliding accident put him out for the rest of the season and it was only through great determination that Patrick qualified his Alfa Romeo on the last row of the grid in Argentina in 1980. Gradually, through Patrick's efforts, the car became competitive and his showings at Long Beach and Monaco proved that Depailler was back, and his claim, that the Alfa would win races by the end of the season, became believable. It was therefore a great tragedy that Formula 1 should lose the talent of the Frenchman forever – for, during testing at Hockenheim on July 1, 1980, his car suddenly veered left coming out of a 165mph right-hander and, sadly, Patrick was killed on impact with a barrier.

For The Record

First GP
1972 France (Tyrrell 004)

GP wins
1978 Monaco (Tyrrell 008)
1979 Spain (Ligier JS 11)

This pleasant American was born on March 18, 1937, in New Jersey. After graduating with a B.Sc. in Mechanical Engineering, Mark started racing with a private Chevrolet Corvette, winning his very first hillclimb. In 1961 he won the 'E Production' Championship in an Elva after a season-long battle with Revson.

Voted 1965 SCCA 'Driver of the Year', after winning two national championships, Mark co-drove Walt Hansgen's Ferrari early in 1966 and then took a place in the Ford Endurance team. After Hansgen's death at Le Mans testing in April, Mark joined forces with Roger Penske to drive an immaculate Group 7 Lola Chevrolet to 2nd place in the inaugural Can-Am series. In 1967 and 1968 he won the American Road Racing Championship and in 1968 also won the Trans-Am series – to be voted SCCA 'Driver of the Year' for the second time.

Starting 1969 well by winning the Daytona 24-hours in a Lola T70, Mark went on to win the Trans-Am title once more, as well as making his Indy debut in a 4-wheel drive Lola. He qualified 4th and ran 3rd until an ignition problem dropped him to 7th – nevertheless he was voted 'Rookie of the Year'.

After finishing 2nd in 1970, Mark

Mark Donohue.

took Indianapolis by storm in 1971, as he qualified 2nd and dominated the race until forced to retire. He won his first USAC race at Pocono and followed this up with an impressive one-off Grand Prix drive in Canada. In a hired McLaren he qualified 8th and soldiered on to finish a fine 3rd in a wet race.

Winning the Indianapolis 500 in 1972 Mark also threatened to walk away with the Can-Am title as well, but for a testing accident in his Porsche at Road Atlanta that put him out of racing for a

Mark's best Grand Prix result came on his debut in a one-off drive at the wet 1971 Canadian Grand Prix – he soldiered on to finish 3rd in a McLaren M19.

time before winning at Edmonton in his comeback drive.

1973 saw Mark totally dominate the whole Can-Am series. Round one saw him tangle with a back-marker to finish 7th. Round two saw him drop to 2nd with a fuel leak. But from then on, Mark and his Porsche 917 won every race! After this success and a 3rd place in the L & M Formula 5000 Championship, Mark announced his retirement after winning the IROC final and that he would be staying with Penske as President and General Manager of the racing operation. However, before the year was out Mark was back in Formula 1 in the new Penske PC1 and racing in the Canadian and United States Grands Prix. After a 7th place in the Argentine Grand Prix, the Penske never proved totally competitive, although Mark picked up a 5th place in Sweden. Back-to-back testing between a Penske and a March 751 persuaded the team to scrap their own car, and in Mark's first race with the March he finished 5th at Silverstone.

However, a month later, on August 17, the car flew off the road during practice at the super-fast Osterreichring and vaulted the guardrail, killing two marshals. As the car had survived the accident remarkaby well, the American was thought to be only mildly concussed. But, sadly, his condition rapidly deteriorated, and, two days later he succumbed to a massive brain haemorrhage. International motor racing had lost one of its most pleasant and skilful drivers.

For The Record

First GP
1971 Canada (McLaren M19)

Best GP Result
3rd 1971 Canada (McLaren M19)

Born on December 12, 1949, Emerson, the son of a motor racing journalist, began his career on motorcycles before moving on to karts and saloons. In 1969 he arrived in England, driving in Formula Ford before being signed-up by Jim Russell for the Formula 3 Lombank Trophy Championship. Emerson had missed the first three races of the series, but this didn't deter him from scoring five victories to take that championship!

In 1970 he was offered a works-supported Lotus 69 Formula 2 car and, after some good placings, which eventually led to his finishing 3rd in the European Formula 2 Championship, Colin Chapman gave Emerson an outdated Lotus 49C for the British Grand Prix which he drove to 8th place. In just two weeks an improvement was obvious, for Emerson took 4th place in the **second** Grand Prix. Disappointment in Austria was followed by a memorable race at Watkins Glen; Emerson winning in only his fourth Grand Prix start. From Formula Ford to winning a Grand Prix in just a year and a half!

All seemed set for a tremendous season with Lotus in 1971, but it was not to be. Emerson's meteoric rise slowed, although he still finished 8th in the Championship and won three Formula 2 races. The 1972 season saw a return to Emerson's earlier form and the wins started in Spain, followed by other successes in Belgium, Britain, Austria and Italy where he secured the World Championship.

Emerson started the 1973 season perfectly, winning the first two races in Argentina and Brazil, finishing 3rd in South Africa, winning again in Spain and adding a 3rd and 2nd in Belgium and Monaco. But failing to score in Sweden and France put Emerson a point behind the incredible Stewart at the halfway point in the Championship. The second half of the season went wrong for Emerson as he only scored one point from the next four races so that his two end-of-season 2nd places were insufficient to retain the title.

A change of teams to McLaren produced a second World

Emerson Fittipaldi.

Championship for Emerson in 1974, but more of a struggle this time in spite of three victories. In the final round at Watkins Glen it was still possible for either Regazzoni or Scheckter to take the title from Emerson, but a smooth, steady 4th place gained him the Championship when both his rivals dropped out.

A good start to the new 1975 season with a win in Argentina and a 2nd place in Brazil as a record the McLaren Team could not maintain, and, with only one more win at a wet Silverstone, Emerson lost his title to the fast, reliable Ferraris.

A shock for the motor racing world was Emerson's decision in 1976 to leave McLaren for his brother's Fittipaldi Team. The new Fittipaldi at first showed promise by qualifying 5th in Brazil, but this really was due to extensive testing at the circuit. For the remainder of the year, and for 1977, Emerson found himself struggling with an uncompetitive car.

The Brazilian GP in 1978 saw a flash of the old Fittipaldi brilliance, when, after qualifying 7th, Emerson finished 2nd to produce the Brazilian's best result ever

Emerson was the revelation of the 1978 Brazilian Grand Prix when he scored a superb 2nd in front of his home crowd in a car bearing his own name.

in a car bearing his own name. After two more dismal seasons Emerson finally decided to call it a day for family reasons, although as director of Fittipaldi Automotive he still appears at the circuits.

Emerson was always a driver who expected high standards of safety as was shown by his withdrawing from the 1975 Spanish and the 1976 Japanese GPs in protest at track conditions. Emerson was always a gentleman, as can be seen by his actions after being punted out of the 1976 Austrian GP by Brambilla. He calmly hopped out of his own stranded car and helped Brambilla out of his cockpit – an action of great courtesy and self-control in the circumstances.

What must be remembered is the successful Fittipaldi of the early Seventies, not the wasted talent of the late Seventies. A truly great driver, a double World Champion, who had a decade in Formula 1.

For The Record

First GP
1970 Britain (Lotus 49C)

GP Wins
1970 United States East (Lotus 72)
1972 Spain (Lotus 72 D)
1972 Belgium (Lotus 72 D)
1972 Britain (Lotus 72 D)
1972 Austria (Lotus 72 D)
1972 Italian (Lotus 72 D)
1973 Argentina (JPS Lotus 72)
1973 Brazil (JPS Lotus 72)
1973 Spain (Lotus 72D)
1974 Brazil (McLaren M23)
1974 Belgium (McLaren M23)
1974 Canada (McLaren M23)
1975 Argentina (McLaren M23)
1975 Britain (McLaren M23)

World Champion
1972 (Lotus)
1974 (McLaren)

Born on Christmas Day 1943, the elder of the two Brazilian racing Fittipaldi brothers, Wilson excelled in many forms of motor sport before Emerson had really begun and, in 1966, he ventured to Europe to drive a Formula 3 Alpine-Renault, but the car never appeared and so he returned home disappointed.

In 1967 Wilson built and prepared a Formula Vee car for Emerson and the following year did the same with a Porsche-engined sports racing car. Emerson went to Britain in 1969 and Wilson followed his trail-blazing brother the next year. Before he left Wilson had already experienced Formula 1 at the wheel of an old Lotus 49 in the non-Championship Argentine Grand Prix. In Britain he bought a Lotus 59 and proved very competitive winning at Montlhery towards the end of 1970 as his brother had done a year earlier. After a series of impressive victories back home in the Brazilian Formula 3 series, Wilson returned to compete in the European Formula 2 – scoring a couple of 4th places.

Beginning 1972 with a 4th in the non-Championship Brazilian GP, Wilson was signed-up for the remainder of the

Wilson Fittipaldi.

season by the Brabham Grand Prix team, making his debut in Spain. Staying with Brabham in 1973, Wilson scored his first World Championship point in Argentina – Emerson won the race! At Monaco came one of the finest drives of

In the 1973 German Grand Prix, Wilson driving a Brabham had the satisfaction of leading his younger brother – Emerson – across the line to finish 5th!

Wilson's career. Having out-qualified team leader Reutemann, Wilson took a secure 3rd place when Ickx retired just after half-distance. However, eight laps from the finish line his engine cut – out of fuel! In Germany Wilson had the satisfaction of leading younger brother Emerson over the line and scoring his best Grand Prix result – 5th.

At the end of the 1973 season Wilson "retired" to concentrate on building an all-Brazilian Formula 1 car. When the Copersucar Fittipaldi FD made its debut in the Argentine Grand Prix it aroused interest, but it soon proved to be disappointingly slow – always qualifying near the back of the grid. Wilson retired again at the end of the year and helped to build a new car for Emerson to drive, without success, in 1976. Although potentially as quick as his brother, Wilson rarely showed his undoubted talent in Formula 1.

For The Record

First GP
1972 Spain (Brabham BT34)

Best GP Result
5th 1973 Germany (Brabham BT 42)

Born on January 27, 1934, this American started his career in the States during the early 1960s racing Porsches but, after the 1961 season, he "retired" only to return to the tracks towards the end of 1964 driving a Porsche-engined Lotus. Victorious in the 1965 United States Road Racing Championship, George moved on to compete in the USAC races from 1967 onwards, as well as competing in long distance Sports, Trans-Am and Can-Am events.

A highly successful 1972 season in which George not only won five races to dominate the Can-Am series in his Penske-Porsche, but won the Trans-Am title as well, led to his being offered a Grand Prix drive with the newly-formed Shadow team in 1973. Scoring a 6th place first time out, in South Africa, and a 3rd on his very next outing, in Spain, flattered to deceive, for these successes were the result of reliability rather than pace – as, sadly, the rest of the season showed.

George Follmer.

In both 1973 and 1974 he finished runner-up in the Can-Am series, and these impressive performances continued when he won no less than eleven of the 1976 Trans-Am rounds, as well as the title. Occasional outings in the 1977 World Championship of Makes, Can-Am and Trans-Am were followed by rare but worthwhile IMSA races with Ongais in a Porsche during 1978. Since then George has competed in a limited number of Can-Am and IMSA events, but with his age now nearing 50, his racing career must surely be at its end.

George's racing career spanned twenty years, and in that time he drove a tremendous variety of machinery – with many worthwhile results!

George scored a surprise 3rd in the 1973 Spanish Grand Prix driving a Shadow, but was unfortunately never a front-runner again.

For The Record

First GP
1973 South Africa (Shadow DN1)

Best GP Result
3rd 1973 Spain (Shadow DN1)

Howden was born on December 24, 1941, in Hamilton, New Zealand. On leaving school in 1957 he became a reporter with a local newspaper, but soon found this to be financially unrewarding and so worked with a construction gang – the object being to obtain sufficient money to participate in motor racing. His first race was in 1960 – he came 2nd! Following a successful 1961 season in a Lotus sports racing car Howden made the journey to Europe in 1963 to race a Ford Falcon in GT races, as well as a Gemini Formula Junior car.

At the end of 1963, in financial difficulties, Howden stopped racing and joined Team McLaren as a mechanic. During 1965 he worked in the United States on the GT XI car, and early in 1966 Howden was loaned by McLaren to Ford where he worked on the transmissions of the Ford Le Mans cars. He then returned to McLaren going to Monaco as mechanic on Bruce McLaren's F1 car.

After that he left McLaren's employ to work in the States on Revson's Can-Am car. Returning to Britain he bought a Brabham Formula 3 car early in 1967 in which he continued his career as a

Howden Ganley.

driver. After several seasons of relatively poor results Howden shot to prominence in the latter races of 1969, setting the first 100mph lap of the Brands Hatch GP circuit in his Chevron B15. Driving a Formula 5000 McLaren for wealthy sponsor Barry Newman, Howden finished 2nd to Gethin in the 1970

Howden speeds round the Karussel at the Nurburgring on his way to a fine 4th place in the 1972 German Grand Prix driving a BRM.

Guards Championship, despite winning only one round at Oulton Park.

Howden's first Formula 1 season with BRM in 1971 showed a considerable record of consistency and, in his last race with the old P153, he finished 2nd in the Oulton Park Gold Cup. On the arrival of the new P160, late in the season, the New Zealander scored his first Grand Prix points for a 5th in Italy – a mere seven tenths of a second behind the winner! He capped the year with a fine 4th place in the States having had to pit for fuel before starting the final lap!

Despite a couple of wins in the 1972 Interserie rounds, Howden's best results in the BRM car were a 4th in Germany and a 6th in Austria. His fortunes in 1973, however, were even worse, for the uncompetitive Iso-Marlboro yielded only a 6th place in Canada.

In 1974 Howden competed only in the two South American races, in a March 741, before leaving Formula 1 for good. In 1975 he joined forces with Tim Schenken to produce a TIGA Formula Ford car for the next season. Designing a variety of cars for the firm Howden has 'been kept busy'. Also, he still competes occasionally in sports cars.

For The Record

First GP
1971 South Africa (BRM P153)

Best GP Result
4th 1971 United States (BRM P160)
4th 1972 Germany (BRM P160)

The ever-smiling Peter Gethin, son of the famous jockey Ken Gethin, was born on February 21, 1940, in Surrey. Peter began racing in a Lotus 7 in 1962 and moved through the ranks of Formula 3 to compete in Formula 2 in 1968.

Forsaking Formula 2, Peter drove in the then new Formula 5000 series in 1969 with great success; winning the first four rounds of the series and the Championship in his McLaren M10A. After dominating the early rounds of the Championship in 1970, Peter was offered a Formula 1 drive with McLaren in the Race of Champions – he came 6th! So when Denny Hulme injured himself testing for Indianapolis, Peter replaced him in the McLaren team and gained a regular drive from the German Grand Prix onwards – scoring a 6th place in Canada in the McLaren M14A. Despite competing in only 13 of the 20 Formula 5000 races he won the Championship and had a win in the Elkhart Lake Can-Am round.

In 1971, despite coming 2nd in the International Trophy at Silverstone, Peter was uncompetitive in the McLaren and so switched to BRM mid-season. In only his second race, at Monza, he won as a jockey's son should win, by a photo-finish (one thousandth of a second)! Fourth at the beginning of the final lap, Peter slipstreamed past Hailwood on the back straight into 3rd place. Peterson led Cevert into the final corner and, both

Peter Gethin.

leaving their braking desperately late, went wide on the exit. Peter by this time had slithered past Cevert and out-accelerated Peterson down the main straight. Peterson attempted to slipstream past Gethin, but left his braking fractionally too late. Peter was victorious – by 24 inches! – and capped the season with a win at the Brands Hatch Victory Race.

After a disappointing 1972 Formula 1 season, in which his best result was a

Peter at speed in his BRM during the 1971 Italian Grand Prix which he won by a thousandth of a second after a dramatic last lap.

6th in Italy, Peter left the Grand Prix world, although he still had one-off drives for BRM and Lola in 1973 and 1974 respectively. Instead, he concentrated on Formula 5000, and in the 1973 Race of Champions made history by being the first driver of a Formula 5000 car to beat a field of combined Formula 1 and Formula 5000 cars.

Peter won the 1974 Tasman Formula 5000 Championship, was runner-up in the 1974 and 1975 European Formula 5000 titles, but had a fruitless 1976 season.

In 1977, however, Peter competed in the Can-Am series and, winning at Road America, was the only driver to challenge the series winner, Tambay. Peter retired at the end of the 1977 season. He will be best remembered for his total domination of Formula 5000 in its early years.

For The Record

First GP
1970 Holland (McLaren M14A)
GP Win
1971 Italy (BRM P160)

The son of a farmer, this cheerful bubbling Italian was born on September 10, 1952, in the Italian province of Brescia. At 17 he was competing in Motorcross events and soon afterwards entered a racing school at Monza. Having competed in the 1972 Italian Formula Ford championship, Bruno's career was delayed by two years of military service. Competing again in 1974, he raced in the Formula Italia series – beating Patrese to win the 1975 Championship. With this title under his belt, Bruno's career moved into top gear when he arrived in England to compete in Formula 3, winning the 1976 Shell Sport series and finishing 2nd in the BP Championship. It was, however, his wins in both the Monaco and the British Grand Prix supporting events that pushed him into the limelight.

Moving to Formula 2 in a private March in 1977, Bruno won at Vallelunga and Mugello. These performances meant he was offered a Grand Prix drive in the third works McLaren at Monza. His impressive GP debut was followed by a runaway Formula 2 win at Donington. This victory proved to be a foretaste of Bruno's total domination of the series in 1978. Arguably his eight victories in the twelve-race series made him one of the most successful Formula 2 drivers of all time. These wins proved to be the right credentials for further occasional Grand Prix drives with McLaren.

Switching to the Alfa Romeo F1 team for 1979, Bruno contributed to the

Bruno Giacomelli.

testing of the brand new car and drove it in its debut race in Belgium, causing surprise by qualifying the hefty machine in the middle of the grid. In 1979 only three more drives materialized for the prototype car, although his drive in Italy – where he took his unwieldy car into 7th place before retirement – deserves special mention.

Competing in his first full season of Grand Prix racing in 1980, Bruno scored points for 5th place in Argentina. Bruno's performance however, was rather mediocre until the leadership of the team was thrust upon the young Italian by Depailler's untimely death. Immediately taking a 5th at Hockenheim – the track where Patrick lost his life – Bruno's performances improved, although good results were thrown away by silly

Although a broken transmission ended a good drive here in the 1981 British Grand Prix, later in the year Bruno scored a competitive 3rd at Las Vegas.

mistakes. Aggressive driving combined with a rapidly improving car led to Bruno setting pole position in the last race of the series at Watkins Glen. From a perfect start he emerged from the season a strong, mature, driver by leading for 32 laps until retirement.

Much was expected of Bruno in 1981 but, after Long Beach and Brazil, the car proved uncompetitive. Uncompetitive, that is, until Italy. There, urged on by his home crowd, Bruno drove a brilliant race to pull his car up into 3rd place until gearbox troubles struck. A 4th in Canada soon after, was followed by a fine 3rd in Las Vegas. Having run 4th early on, Bruno spun but fought back through the field passing Patrese, Reutemann, Piquet, Mansell and, so nearly, Prost. An exceptional performance that bodes well for 1982....

For The Record

First GP
1977 Italy (McLaren M23)
Best GP Result
3rd 1981 Las Vegas (Alfa Romeo 179C)

Born on 4th April 1940 Mike Hailwood was, quite simply, the greatest racing motor cyclist of all time – he was **ten times world champion!** A record further enhanced when he returned to the Isle of Man in 1978, after an absence of ten years, and won a production motorcycle race, repeating the achievement the next year!

Mike had two spells in Formula 1 racing, the first beginning in 1963 with two drives in a Lotus-Climax for Reg Parnell after racing Brabham Formula Juniors. A full Grand Prix season the following year brought Mike only a single Championship point, at Monaco, in a Lotus-BRM. After one more race in 1965, Mike returned to bikes. However, he had occasional Sports Car races, and even came 3rd at Le Mans in 1969, before deciding to return to car racing fulltime, driving in Formula 5000 with great verve. Racing a Lola in 1969 and 1970 he came 3rd and 4th in the F5000 Championship.

After a very successful 1971 Formula 5000 season in a Surtees TS8, scoring four wins to take 2nd place in the Championship, Mike was offered a Surtees Formula 1 drive in the Italian Grand Prix. His comeback drive was impressive – from 17th on the grid he

Mike Hailwood.

was in the lead by lap 25 but finished 4th in a four-car storming finish, just 0.18 seconds behind the winner! Another good outing in the States encouraged Surtees to sign up Mike for a whole season in 1972.

Although he achieved a 2nd place at Monza, and three other placings among the top six, Mike was unlucky. Both in the

A 2nd at Monza in 1972, driving a Surtees, was Mike's best Grand Prix result, although he was unfortunate not to emerge victorious in other events.

South African Grand Prix and in the International Trophy Race at Silverstone he was challenging for the lead when mechanical failure struck. He did, however, pick up a 2nd place in the Race of Champions at Brands Hatch. Mike was more successful in other formulae. In the Tasman Formula 5000 series he finished 2nd and in Formula 2 he won the European Championship with two outright wins and three non-graded wins.

A season of accidents and mechanical failures followed in 1973, leaving Mike without a solitary point; although he had gained the George Medal for heroically saving Regazzoni from his burning BRM in South Africa. So for 1974 Mike switched to McLaren gaining 4th, 5th and 3rd places in the first three races of the season; putting him equal-2nd in the World Championship, one point behind Regazzoni. However, only a 4th in Holland followed before a terrible accident at the Nurburgring. "Landing" badly after rounding the notorious Pflanzgarten corner, Mike's car went nose first into a guardrail and he suffered severe leg injuries. After a long and painful fight back to mobility Mike decided to call it a day in mid-1975.

It was with great sadness that the motor racing world learnt of Mike's death on Monday March 23, 1981, after a tragic car crash on the public highway near his home which also claimed his young daughter.

For The Record

First GP
1963 Britain (Lotus-Climax)

Best GP result
2nd 1972 Italy (Surtees TS9B)

Norman Graham Hill was a great ambassador for the sport of motor racing. He was a most versatile driver and the only one to win the 'Triple Crown'. That is the World Championship (1962 and 1968), Indianapolis (1966) and Le Mans (1972). Born February 15, 1929, Graham started racing late in life – after an apprenticeship with Smiths Instruments and two years of National Service in the Navy – when he paid 5 shillings a lap to drive a racing car round Brands Hatch. He was hooked! Graham tried to obtain drives in exchange for working as a mechanic, and even set up a motor racing school.

He made his debut racing appearance in April 1954 in a Formula 3 Cooper at Brands Hatch and came 4th. After this he met Colin Chapman and went to work fulltime for Lotus, having the occasional 1956 race in a Lotus II. Graham drove briefly for the Cooper works team in 1957 before returning to Chapman as a works Lotus driver.

In 1958 Graham made his Grand Prix debut at Monaco in a Lotus 12, where he ran 4th until a rear wheel fell off! However, the car was unreliable, so, at the end of 1959, he switched to the BRM team, finishing 3rd in the 1960

Graham Hill.

Dutch GP. After a rather dismal 1961 season in which his best position was 5th (at Watkins Glen), Graham, in the new BRM P57, won the pre-season meetings at Goodwood and Silverstone, going on to win four Grands Prix **and** the 1962 World Championship!

He was runner-up for the next three years, each year winning at Monaco and Watkins Glen. It is interesting to note that in 1964 Graham scored more points than Surtees, but lost the Championship by

Graham showed his enthusiasm for the sport by setting up his own team, whose car he is seen driving here, in the early Seventies.

one point because of the points scoring system! The new BRM H16 engine proved troublesome during 1966, so Graham returned to Lotus for the 1967 season but only managed two second places.

In 1968 it was a different story, for Graham won in Spain, Monaco and Mexico to take the hard fought 1968 title. 1969 was notable in two ways for Graham; firstly he won his fifth Monaco GP in seven years; secondly, at Watkins Glen Graham had a nasty accident when a tyre deflated, throwing him out of the car and breaking both his legs. After a tremendous effort to get fit again, Graham, against doctors' advice, insisted on racing in the 1970 South African GP, coming 6th in Rob Walker's private Lotus, in an otherwise poor season. Graham never seemed to be as competitive after his 1969 shunt and the only notable result of two years driving for Brabham in 1971-2 was the winning of the non-Championship International Trophy race at Silverstone.

After setting up his own Formula 1 team for the 1973 season, Graham only scored three points in three years racing! As a result he decided to retire midway through the 1975 season, realising that with youngsters around quicker than himself it was not fair to hog the cockpit. Retirement enabled Graham to concentrate on his new team and cars. However, on November 19, 1976 while returning to Elstree Aerodrome from testing the new Hill GH2 at Paul Ricard,

Graham's plane crashed on Arkley Golf Course in North London. Tragically, Graham and his five passengers were killed.

Graham Hill had raced for 22 years, 18 of which had been spent in Formula 1. He achieved this incredible feat by sheer dedication and determined hard work. It was bitterly tragic that this highly popular British driver should be killed within months of retiring from his beloved sport.

For The Record

First GP
1958 Monaco (Lotus 12)

GP Wins
1962 Holland (BRM P57)
1962 Germany (BRM (P57)
1962 Italy (BRM P57)
1962 South Africa (BRM P57)
1963 Monaco (BRM P57)
1963 United States (BRM P61)
1964 Monaco (BRM P261)
1964 United States (BRM P261)
1965 Monaco (BRM P261)
1965 United States (BRM P261)
1968 Spain (Lotus 49)
1968 Monaco (Lotus 49)
1968 Mexico (Lotus 49B)
1969 Monaco (Lotus 49B)

World Champion
1962 (BRM)
1968 (Lotus)

Denny Hulme was born on June 18, 1936. This tough, likeable New Zealander started racing with class wins in local hillclimbs with an MG. After the 1958 New Zealand Grand Prix he bought a 2-litre Cooper-Climax, winning the 'Driver to Europe' scholarship with the car in 1960. Once in Europe, Denny drove Coopers in Formula Junior, Formula 2 and finally in Formula 1; the latter in a brief debut at Snetterton on a limited budget. However this paid off, and Denny won seven out of his fourteen races in Formula Junior for the Brabham team in 1963, and had a Formula 1 ride at Karlskora in Sweden. Denny was then elevated to the new Formula 2 team, proving himself to be as fast as 'Black Jack' Brabham on occasions.

Moving up into Formula 1 in 1965, Denny scored his first World Championship points for a fine 4th place in France, before becoming Brabham's regular Number 2 in 1966 and 1967. In 1967 he won his first Grand Prix at Monaco where he had made his debut two years earlier, and went on to win both the German race and the World Championship!.

In 1968 Denny joined the McLaren

Denny Hulme.

team and won the Can-Am Championship but, despite two late-season victories in Italy and Canada, he could only manage 3rd place in the World Championship. The "never-say-die" New Zealander was deeply

Denny's McLaren M23 in the wet during 1974 – a year he crowned with a victory in Argentina.

distressed when his firm friend Bruce McLaren was tragically killed in a testing accident in 1970, and it was Denny who pulled the McLaren team through, by winning the Can-Am Championship again.

Unfortunate to drop back during the 1971 South African Grand Prix due to a suspension fault, when comfortably leading, Denny made amends by scoring a fortunate victory in the same event the next year.

Staying with McLaren until announcing his retirement at the end of 1974, further victories materialized in Sweden 1973 and Argentina 1974. His close contact with the fatal Cevert and Revson accidents persuaded him to drive within his capabilities during his final season, which was still very quickly! 'The Bear', as Denny was known because of his stocky appearance, was a fighting, persevering, yet sometimes underrated driver.

For The Record

First GP
1965 Monaco (Brabham BT11)

GP Wins
1967 Monaco (Brabham BT20)
1967 Germany (Brabham BT24)
1968 Italy (McLaren M7A)
1968 Canada (McLaren M7A)
1969 Mexico (McLaren M7A)
1972 South Africa (McLaren (M19A)
1973 Sweden (McLaren (M23)
1974 Argentina (McLaren M23)

World Champion
1967 (Brabham)

This colourful, controversial Public School boy was born on August 29, 1947. Although he competed in Junior Wimbledon tennis and was a squash player of county class, James decided to race, first Minis, then, in 1968 Formula Ford cars. Despite beginning 1969 in Formula Ford, by the end of the year he was a top name in Formula 3, with some fine performances earning him the Grovewood Award.

1970 saw James in a Formula 3 Lotus 59, and being impressive enough for March to sign him on for their Formula 3 team in 1971, scoring a number of useful victories. Dropped by March in mid-season 1972, James joined a small outfit backed by Lord Hesketh. After a series of late-season Formula 2 and Formule Libre races in an old March 712, the Northamptonshire peer decided to move his team into Formula 1.

James's first competitive Formula 1 drive came in the Brands Hatch Race of Champions where he came 3rd in a leased Surtees. The team's Grand Prix debut was at Monaco using a March 731 and they surprised many by running 6th until retirement. From then on results just improved and improved! A 6th in France, despite losing an air scoop a few laps from the end; 4th with fastest lap, in Britain (a 3rd until James had to give way to Hulme with three laps to go) 3rd after another outstanding drive in Holland. And, in the States, a superb 2nd place having passed Reutemann and put relentless pressure on Peterson, setting fastest lap in the process. The achievements of the immaculately prepared March must have surpassed even the team's most wildly optimistic hopes.

The new Hesketh 308 boosted the team's ego even further when they won the International Trophy at their 'home circuit' of Silverstone. 3rd places in Sweden and Austria followed despite a series of retirements in between. The season ended on a high note, with a 4th in Canada and a 3rd at Watkins Glen. In fact the latter was to have been 2nd until

James Hunt.

both brake and fuel problems intervened...

In the 1975 Argentinian GP, James took the lead at half-distance, but the team had to wait until Holland for that long-awaited Grand Prix victory – beating the Ferraris of Lauda and Regazzoni in a wet race! Two weeks later James was 2nd in France and in Austria 2nd again, after leading for a number of laps. Despite a late season run of good results which pushed James up to 4th in the Championship, Hesketh failed to attract sponsorship and the team folded. James, his talent recognised, was immediately snapped-up to lead the McLaren team in 1976.

In Brazil, the first race of the 1976 season, James set the first of what was to be eight pole positions that year. After a 2nd in South Africa, James' first win for McLaren came in Spain. This venue also signified the start of the political wrangling that was to mar a glorious year; James was disqualified as the car was said to be too wide, but was later reinstated.

A 5th place in Sweden (Round 7) left James an enormous 47 points behind Lauda – and surely no hope of the title! However, wins in France, Britain (although he was later ruled ineligible for the restart after a first corner accident), Germany, Holland, Canada and the United States – as well as Lauda's

James, the talented 1976 World Champion, competing in a Wolf during 1979 – his final season before retirement.

accident – put James a mere three points behind the Austrian as they met for the final race of the Championship in Japan. Here, leading for the first 60 laps, James seemed certain to take the title as Lauda had retired. But weather conditions necessitated a late tyre change, dropping him to 5th place! Two points were not enough, with four laps to go! Somehow, though, James managed to pull up to 3rd at the finish, **to take the Championship by just one point!** As if to prove his ascendancy, James also won the Race of Champions and the International Trophy.

A series of frustrating races early in 1977 put the title beyond the reach of James. Even so his Silverstone victory was suberb – as were his wins in the States and Japan. The fact that he also set six pole positions proved that James was still a force to be reckoned with. However, there were to be no more victories for, with the advent of the ground-effects Lotus 79, McLaren found themselves floundering in 1978 even though James finished a hard-charging 3rd in France.

1979 was to be James' last season, a season to be remembered. Sadly, in a Wolf, the dream was never realised – despite showing his old form on occasions. Two weeks after Monaco James decided to quit, feeling that drivers were now less important than designers when it came to winning races ...

James was a worthy winner of the 1976 title and, deservedly, will be remembered as a top class racing driver whilst we listen to his succinct Grand Prix commentaries based on the wealth of his own experience.

For The Record

First GP
1973 Monaco (March 731)

GP Wins
1975 Holland (Hesketh 308)
1976 Spain (McLaren M23)
1976 France (McLaren M23)
1976 *Britain (McLaren M23)
1976 Germany (Mclaren M23)
1976 Holland (McLaren M23)
1976 Canada (McLaren M23)
1976 United States (McLaren M23)
1977 Britain (McLaren M26)
1977 United States (McLaren M26)
1977 Japan (McLaren M26)
*Later disqualified, the race going to Niki Lauda.

World Champion
1976 (McLaren)

Jacky Ickx, the son of a famous Belgian motoring journalist, was born on New Year's Day 1945. Three times Belgian Trials Champion, Jacky started hillclimbing at 17. In 1964, while racing a Lotus Cortina, Jacky met Ken Tyrrell who offered him a Formula 3 drive. Unable to accept the offer at first because of National Service, Jacky eventually had a trial in a Cooper Formula 2 car at the end of 1965, after which he signed a 3-year contract.

A season plagued by mechanical failures was followed in 1967 by three wins which were enough to give Jacky the European Formula 2 Championship. He had his first taste of Formula 1 when he stood in for the injured Pedro Rodriguez of the Cooper team, and finished 6th in the Italian Grand Prix at Monza.

The young Belgian was to have raced in the Tyrrell-run Matra Formula 1 team in 1968, but eventually signed for Ferrari. A string of mid-season successes including two 4ths, three 3rds and a victory in France, proved that Jacky was a top line Formula 1 driver.

Switching to Brabham for 1969, Jacky totally dominated both the German and the Canadian events from pole position and had many other good results – notably 2nds in Britain and Mexico – eventually finishing 2nd to Stewart in the World Championship.

Returning to Ferrari in 1970, Jacky scored only a 3rd place in the first half of the season. However, in the second half, he scored a 2nd in Germany and a 1st in Austria. After winning in Canada Jacky looked set to win again in the United States, but he had to pit to replace a broken fuel pipe, and eventually finished 4th – although he ended the season with a fine win in Mexico. It is interesting to note that if he hadn't pitted in the United States GP, Jacky would have been World Champion instead of Rindt.

An early season run of 2nd, 3rd and 1st put Jacky just five points behind Stewart in the 1971 title chase, but unfortunately, those were the last points he scored that year. Although Jacky often featured high up in the 1972 lap

Jacky Ickx.

charts, he only won in Germany, despite four pole positions and three fastest laps. However, six Ferrari Sports Car wins boosted his morale. By mid-1973 it became clear that Jacky was unhappy at Ferrari and so when they didn't enter in Germany he raced for McLaren to produce his best result of the year – a 3rd place.

After leaving Ferrari, Jacky had only moderate success in Formula 1. In 1974 he picked up a couple of 3rds, in Brazil and Britain, in an outdated Lotus, staying with the team during 1975 to finish in the points only once – with a 2nd in the accident-shortened Spanish Grand Prix.

Despite a 3rd in the Race of Champions with a Williams, and a late season switch to Ensign, Jacky failed to score a point in 1976. After having an occasional race with Ensign in 1977 and 1978, Jacky was offered a top-line Formula 1 drive in the Ligier team midway through 1979 to replace the injured Depailler. Jacky, past his heyday, failed to really impress, scoring only a 6th and a 5th – and instead tried to find success in Sports Car racing.

Having already won Le Mans in 1969 (Ford GT40), 1975 (Ford GR8),

Jacky – one of the masters of the Nurburgring – scored his last Grand Prix win in a Ferrari during a dominant display in the 1972 event.

1976 and 1977 (Porsche 936), Jacky was attempting to win the race for a record-breaking fifth time. In 1978 he had finished 2nd, in 1979 he retired while figuring strongly and at the end of the year he supposedly retired from motor-racing only to return to Le Mans for a one-off drive in 1980, finishing a frustrating 2nd. Once again returning from 'retirement' Jacky finally achieved his ambition when he dominated the 1981 race with Derek Bell to score an incredible fifth win!

Jacky was, indeed, unfortunate not to be credited with the title 'World Champion' as he was often the fastest man on the Grand Prix circuits in the period 1968 to 1972. Jacky notched up more international Sports Car racing victories than any other driver – and five

wins at Le Mans is a tremendous achievement!

A man who enjoyed his racing... so will Le Mans lure him back yet again?

For The Record

First GP
1967 Italy (Cooper T81B-Maserati)

GP wins
1968 France (Ferrari 312)
1969 Germany (Brabham BT26)
1969 Canada (Brabham BT26)
1970 Austria (Ferrari 312B)
1970 Canada (Ferrari 312B)
1970 Mexico (Ferrari 312B)
1971 Holland (Ferrari 312B2)
1972 Germany (Ferrari 312B2)

This tall, blond Frenchman was born on October 1 1942. He began racing a Renault R8 saloon in 1966 before moving up to Formula 3. Here he stayed for several seasons twice finishing 2nd in the French Championship, with his brother-in-law Jacques Laffite acting as his mechanic.

Into Formula 2 in 1974, Jean-Pierre won at Hockenheim to take 4th place in the final Championship positions. Jean-Pierre also came 3rd in the European 2-litre Sports Car Championship. Despite winning the Formula 2 race at the Salzburgring in 1975, Jean-Pierre could only finish 5th in the Championship. He was obviously impressive as both Williams and Surtees gave him tries in Grand Prix cars, but Jean-Pierre failed to qualify. In France, though, driving the third Tyrrell he qualified and finished 12th in the race.

1976 was Jean-Pierre's year in Formula 2, as he consistently finished in the points, winning at Vallelunga and Mugello. However, he still went into the final round at Hockenheim behind Rene Arnoux in points, but sealed the Championship when he won the race from pole position.

After much testing by Jean-Pierre the Formula 1 Renault Turbo finally

Jean-Pierre Jabouille.

made its debut at Silverstone to race in the final few races of the 1977 season – the car proving unreliable. 1978 saw a gradual increase in competitiveness – but not in reliability – until Jean-Pierre finally took his first points in Formula 1 for a 4th place at Watkins Glen.

Nothing much changed as far as results were concerned in 1979, despite a pole position in South Africa where the altitude of the track aids the turbo-

In Austria Jean-Pierre scored his only Grand Prix points of the 1980 season with Renault – but he won the race which was some consolation!

charger, until the new ground-effects RS 11 arrived. With it Jean-Pierre immediately took pole position and won in the team's home Grand Prix at Dijon!

Jean-Pierre dominated the early part of 1980 when he set pole position and led in both Brazil and South Africa before being forced to retire. A late season run of four consecutive front row positions gave Jean-Pierre his second and last Grand Prix win of his career – in Austria. However, a suspension failure at the end of the year pitched Jean-Pierre headlong into an Armco barrier from which he suffered multiple fractures to his right leg – an injury that would eventually shorten his Grand Prix career.

After three and a half years with Renault, Jean-Pierre moved to Talbot-Ligier for 1981, possibly in an attempt to gain reliability, but even after a long recovery Jean-Pierre was never a match for his team-mate Laffite and, after the Spanish Grand Prix, he retired.

It is unfortunate that Jean-Pierre's career should have ended in such a way as, undoubtedly, he was one of the very best test drivers around. Mechanical unreliability spoiled excellent drives, especially in 1980, when Jean-Pierre led no less than five Grands Prix. At Le Mans he has set pole position but has never won.

Jean-Pierre remains at Talbot-Ligier as technical adviser.

For The Record

First GP
1975 France (Tyrrell 007)

GP wins
1979 France (Renault RS 11)
1980 Austria (Renault RE 23)

Sometimes brilliant, sometimes mediocre, this experienced but inconsistent French star was born on July 10, 1946. His motor-racing career began when he raced Renault R8 saloons while at university in 1967. Competing in Formula France single-seaters the following year, Jean-Pierre moved up to Formula 3 in 1969. In 1971 he handled a Formula 2 March, scoring two fine 3rd places before making a lack-lustre Grand Prix debut at Monza in a rented March.

His real break came when March signed him on to spearhead both their Formula 1 and their Formula 2 teams in 1973. Although disappointing in Formula 1, Jean-Pierre was all-conquering in Formula 2 – notching up seven outright wins and taking the Championship.

Signed-up by Shadow for 1974, he became team leader after Revson's early season accident. At Monaco Jean-Pierre drove with impressive fire to finish 3rd, although he clipped the Armco on the last corner when distracted by the crowd! Two weeks later, he was on fine form again – this time in Sweden – although brake problems forced him back to 5th. A string of mechanical troubles marred the rest of the season although Jean-Pierre scored five impressive Sports Car victories in a shared Matra-Simca.

On brilliant form in Argentina 1975, Jean-Pierre set pole position, only to

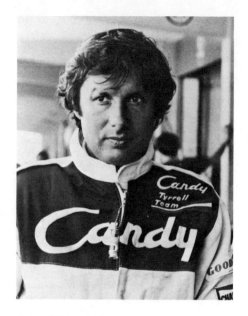

Jean-Pierre Jarier.

retire on the warm-up lap. Brazil again saw him on pole with the new Shadow. This time he simply disappeared from the rest of the field, building-up a lead of nearly half a minute, before the fuel metering unit broke! The highlight of an otherwise disappointing season: Jean-Pierre had to be content with a new lap record.

A year later, in Brazil again, Jean-Pierre was placed 2nd and had closed within two seconds of the leader before

Upon joining the Osella team at the 1981 British Grand Prix, Jean-Pierre immediately showed his ability by making what had been an uncompetitive car into a regular mid-field runner.

spinning off on oil with a mere seven laps to go – the "Jarier Jinx" had struck again! However, as the Shadow became less competitive, so did the Frenchman and he was lucky to land the ATS-Penske drive in 1977, scoring first time out with a 6th place at Long Beach. Occasional races for Shadow, Ligier and ATS followed.

Peterson's fatal Monza crash gave Jean-Pierre the chance to prove his brilliance again – this time in the Lotus team. In the States he pitted early in the race and dropped to 21st but, within 25 laps, he rocketed up the field to 5th, and, breaking the lap record, was soon 3rd before retiring – out of fuel – with less than four laps to go. A week later saw Jean-Pierre on pole in Canada. Giving a superb demonstration of skill in a solitary romp at the head of the field, he built up a tremendous lead before being forced to retire with victory in sight....

Consistent in 1979, Jean-Pierre led the Tyrrell team, scoring an impressive 3rd in South Africa after an exciting battle with Andretti. Good drives at Long Beach, Jarama, Dijon and Silverstone gave him his best World Championship placing with 14 points.

A poor 1980 season, with Tyrrell, yielded only three 5th places, and so, despite hoping to land a regular Lotus drive, Jean-Pierre was left without a drive at the start of 1981. An unfit Jabouille allowed him to take the number two seat at Ligier for the season's first two races. Long Beach saw Jean-Pierre qualify a superb 2nd in the first session, and in Brazil he ran 6th until waving team leader Laffite past near the end.

Asked to drive the uncompetitive Osella in Britain, Jean-Pierre immediately showed his experience by making the car a regular midfield runner – although his team-mate still failed to qualify!

As has been shown in South America in 1975, and North America in 1978, given a good car Jean-Pierre is unbeatable. It seems criminal that he has not, at least, one Grand Prix win to his credit, but there is time yet!

For The Record

First GP
1971 Italy (March 701)

Best GP result
3rd 1974 Monaco (Shadow DN3)
3rd 1979 South Africa (Tyrrell 009)
3rd 1979 Britain (Tyrrell 009)

A tough, hard fighter, this highly acclaimed racing driver was born on November 2, 1946, the son of the successful Australian driver Stan Jones. Beginning his racing career whilst still a teenager, he won the 1963 Australian Karting Championship before financial problems forced him to quit the sport for a while.

Resurfacing in 1970, he came to Britain to compete in Formula 3. Selling second-hand cars to make ends meet, it was not until 1973 that he proved his potential by finishing runner-up in the series, a mere two points behind Tony Brise.

A well-spent Formula Atlantic season, in 1974, prompted Alan's sponsors to buy an ex-works Formula 1 Hesketh but, after a few fruitless outings, his sponsors withdrew. Even so, Alan secured a drive with the Hill team – replacing an injured Stommelen and scoring a 5th in Germany. The man to beat in Formula 5000 by the end of the year, Alan was signed up by Surtees in 1976 and showed flashes of inspiration

Alan Jones

on occasions – notably when he finished 2nd behind Hunt in the Brands Hatch Race of Champions.

Joining Shadow in 1977 after Pryce's untimely death early in the season, Alan – although never spectacular in practice – often shone in the race; no more so than in Austria

Alan was desperately unlucky not to have secured the World Title for a second time in 1981. Here at Silverstone he prepares to leave the pits in his Williams during practice for the British Grand Prix.

where he had a truly amazing charge through the field from 14th on the grid to 2nd place by lap 16! This forceful drive paid off when Hunt retired leaving Alan to score his own, and Shadow's, first Grand Prix win. A similar drive, this time resulting in a 3rd place, followed in Italy.

Desperately unlucky in 1978, especially when challenging for the lead at Long Beach (where he set fastest lap), and Brands Hatch, Alan nevertheless managed to salvage a 2nd at Watkins Glen for the new-look Williams team, as well as dominating the Can-Am Championship.

The new FW07 arrived midway into the 1979 season; its potential was first really demonstrated by Alan's shattering practice lap at Silverstone. Although forced to retire in the race, he went on to score a hat-trick of wins in Germany, Austria and Holland, and added a further victory in Canada. However, his challenge came too late to wrest the title from Scheckter but in 1980 he made no mistake. Starting the year with a win from pole position in Argentina, he went on to dominate the second half of the season winning in France, Britain, Canada and the United States to achieve the World Championship.

Refusing to rest on his laurels, Alan was determined, not only to defend, but to hang on to his World Championship title in 1981. Unfortunately, a misfire at Monaco and Hockenheim lost the talented Australian certain wins and, ultimately, the title. Following up his earlier victory at Long Beach, Alan – having already announced his intention to retire – was determined to go out with a bang! This he certainly did, for in his last Grand Prix in Las Vegas he was untouchable – leading from start to finish!

So nearly pulling off a World Championship double – but eventually finishing a mere four points behind the 1981 Champion, Piquet – Alan is a driver never satisfied unless he is giving his personal best. His retirement has left a chasm in the world of Formula 1 now he has returned to his farm outside Melbourne. However, many feel that Alan's "retirement" is not of the permanent type....

For The Record

First GP
1975 Spain (Hesketh 308)

GP Wins
1977 Austria (Shadow DN8)
1979 Germany (Williams FW07)
1979 Austria (Williams FW07)
1979 Holland (Williams FW07)
1979 Canada (Williams FW07)
1980 Argentina (Williams FW07)
1980 France (Williams FW07B)
1980 Britain (Williams FW07B)
1980 Canada (Williams FW07B)
1980 United States, East
(Williams FW07B)
1981 United States, West
(Williams FW07C)
1981 Las Vegas (Williams FW07C)

World Champion
1980 (Williams)

Jacques-Henri Laffite was born on November 21, 1943, the son of a lawyer. The cheerful Frenchman first came into contact with motor racing when he acted as a mechanic for his brother-in-law Jean-Pierre Jabouille. But soon, he too wished to race and so attended a racing drivers' school in 1969, before going on to win the Formula Renault Championship in 1972.

1973 saw Jacques emerge as one of the top European Formula 3 drivers, winning the French Championship as well as the Monaco race. Into Formula 2 the following year, Jacques showed sufficient prowess to be invited to race for the Williams Grand Prix team by mid-season.

European Formula 2 Champion in 1975 with a superb run of early season victories, Jacques crowned his year by scoring a fine 2nd place in the German Grand Prix, when the front runners hit trouble. However, these were the only points he scored all season so he did not hesitate to join the brand new Ligier Formula 1 team for 1976. Although not a regular front-runner, Jacques surprised many during the year – especially when he set pole position for the Italian Grand Prix!

It was not, however, until the Swedish event the following year that he scored his first Grand Prix win. Although

Jacques Laffite.

8th on the grid, Jacques found his car to be handling superbly in the race-day warm-up and so, when the lights switched to green at the start, he quickly moved up through the field to take the lead a couple of laps from the end when Andretti pitted! Further good drives followed in Holland and Japan, but 1978 failed to produce the results he had

Consistent mid-season points scoring during 1981 – like his 3rd here in the British Grand Prix – allowed Jacques a crack at the title at the end of the year in his Talbot-Ligier.

hoped for even though he finished 3rd in Spain and Germany.

With Ligier's switch to using Cosworth rather than Matra engines in 1979, Jacques totally dominated and won both the South American Races. The motor-racing world started to think of Jacques as becoming the new World Champion, but it was not to be, for, although Ligier threatened to run away with the Spanish and Belgian races the results were not forthcoming and three consecutive 3rds only remotely kept his Championship hopes alive.

A regular front-runner in 1980, it was not until the French and British GPs that Jacques really looked a certain winner. But, whereas in those events he was let down by his car when he so deserved to win, in Germany he won unexpectedly!

Back with Matra engines for 1981, the Ligiers were at first midfield runners but, with the arrival of the European season, Jacques became a consistent points scorer and with wins in Austria and Canada he was even able to have a shot at the title in the final race of the season at Las Vegas. Typically, Jacques gave the race all he'd got, but having pushed his car up to 2nd place, his chances were spoilt by a late stop for fresh tyres.

A tough, aggressive, driver when the need arises, Jacques – the popular Frenchman – is a proven race winner and can, therefore, never be overlooked as a possible candidate for the World Championship...

For The Record

First GP
1974 Germany (Williams FW02)

GP Wins
1977 Sweden (Ligier JS7)
1979 Argentina (Ligier JS11)
1979 Brazil (Ligier JS11)
1980 Germany (Ligier JS11/15)
1981 Austria (Talbot-Ligier JS17)
1981 Canada (Talbot-Ligier JS17)

Niklaus Andreas "Niki" Lauda was born on February 22, 1949, and began his career when he competed in hillclimbs in 1968 with a Cooper 1300, and then a Porsche 911, before moving on to Kaimann Formula V by the end of the season.

Niki quickly moved up the motor racing "ladder" competing in a Formula 3 McNamara in 1970, coming 2nd at Brno, Czechoslovakia. He entered March's "rent-a-drive" Formula 2 team in 1971, coming 6th at the Nurburgring, 4th at Rouen and made an impressive Formula 1 debut in his native Austrian Grand Prix in the same year! He continued his rise in Formula 1 during 1972. He borrowed £35,000 from an Austrian bank to become No. 2 to Ronnie Peterson in the March team, but his best

Niki Lauda.

Although disastrous in Niki's terms, his 1979 season produced many excellent drives such as at Monaco where he held a strong 3rd in his Brabham-Alfa until forced to retire.

result of the year came in the Oulton Park Formula 2 race which he won.

Joining the BRM team in 1973, as No. 3 driver to Regazzoni and Beltoise, gained Niki his first points in Formula 1 when he came 5th in Belgium. He also ran a fighting 3rd at Monaco, only to retire. These impressive performances caught the eye of the Ferrari team and he was signed-up to spearhead a revitalised Ferrari Formula 1 attack, alongside Regazzoni, in 1974. During the 1974 season the slightly built, youthful, toothy Austrian put his car on pole position for nine of that year's fifteen Grands Prix. He led eight, and won two!

In 1975 the picture was more complete, as Lauda again took nine pole positions but this time out of only fourteen Grands Prix, and won five of them to become World Champion driver.

The 1976 season started perfectly for Lauda as he won five out of the first six Grands Prix, and came 2nd in the other! However, triumph turned to disaster at the Nurburgring during the German GP. His Ferrari went out of control during the race, crashed and burst into flames. Miraculously, Niki was rescued by fellow drivers and taken to hospital suffering from the effects of fumes and severe burns. In fact he was in such a critical condition that last rites were administered, but his determination and fitness pulled him from death's door and, only six weeks later, he came 4th in the Italian Grand Prix!

Although losing his title to James Hunt in 1976, in 1977 Niki won his second World Championship with a tremendously reliable car, finishing in the top three ten times. However, by the end of the season, Niki had grown tired of Ferrari politics and so moved on to Brabham for the 1978 season.

1978 was quite successful, with two controversial wins going to Niki in a Lotus dominated season. Following a disastrous 1979 season, in the Brabham BT48, Niki coolly announced his retirement from racing midway through practice for the Canadian GP: he was 'tired of driving around in circles.'

On "retirement" Niki set up his own airline 'Lauda Air' but, to the delight of motor-racing fans, has announced his return to Grand Prix racing in 1982, this time with the McLaren International team. A surprising move that will, assuredly, bring further success to this highly skilled and tactical driver.

For The Record

First GP
1971 Austria (March 711)

GP Wins
1974 Spain (Ferrari 312B3)
1974 Holland (Ferrari 312B3)
1975 Monaco (Ferrari 312T)
1975 Belgium (Ferrari 312T)
1975 Sweden (Ferrari 312T)
1975 France (Ferrari 312T)
1975 United States (Ferrari 312T)
1976 Brazil (Ferrari 312T)
1976 South Africa (Ferrari 312T)
1976 Spain (Ferrari 312T2)
1976 Belgium (Ferrari 312T2)
1976 Monaco (Ferrari 312T2)
1976* Britain (Ferrari 312T2)
1977 South Africa (Ferrari 312T2)
1977 Germany (Ferrari 312T2)
1977 Holland (Ferrari 312T2)
1978 Sweden (Brabham BT46B)
1978 Italy (Brabham BT46)

* 'Won' on the disqualification of James Hunt

World Champion
1975 and 1977 (Ferrari)

This Dutch driver was born on March 16, 1942, and began his racing career in 1963. He raced Formula Vee but, eventually, was to make his name in Sports Car racing. After some impressive outings during 1970 in a Porsche 908, Gijs proved his consistency and faultless driving when he won at Le Mans in 1971 with Marko. Offered a works Surtees, even though it was the outdated TS7, Gijs made his Grand Prix debut in front of his home crowd. In a great effort he ran 8th from lap 28 of the 70 lap race before finishing the year with a 2nd in the Watkins Glen 6-hour Sports Car race.

Racing Formula 5000 in 1972, Gijs' consistent drives took him into the lead of the European Championship by mid-season and, with just two wins, he took the title by a narrow margin.

Once again he raced in his home Grand Prix in 1973, this time in an Iso Marlboro. He came 6th to score his first World Championship point in a typically steady drive. In Formula 5000 he never looked like retaining his title, but in Sports Cars he had a fine win in the Targa Florio and a 4th at Le Mans.

1974 saw just one Grand Prix drive in Belgium, for Iso Marlboro. In a Porsche Carrera Turbo he had good

Gijs van Lennep.

results at Spa (3rd), Le Mans (2nd) and Watkins Glen (2nd). Replacing the injured Wunderink in the Ensign Team, Gijs competed in the 1975 Dutch, French and German Grands Prix, inheriting 6th in the latter.

1976 saw more success for Gijs at Le Mans in his last motor race before retirement. With the incredible Ickx he notched up his second victory in the

Gijs replaced the injured Wunderink at Ensign during the mid-season 1975 Grands Prix; inheriting 6th place at the Nurburgring.

event with a Porsche 936 Turbo. What a swansong!

Gijs' great asset was his invariably faultless driving. It was this that made him such a successful Sports Car driver, although he perhaps lacked that extra fire needed to make him a Grand Prix Champion.

For The Record

First GP
1971 Holland (Surtees TS7)

Best GP Result
6th 1973 Holland (Iso Marlboro IR-01)
6th 1975 Germany (Ensign N175)

"The Tigress of Turin" was born in Turin on March 26, 1943, the daughter of a butcher. Having proved herself moderately successful in Formula Monza and Formula 3, Lella surprised many by proving remarkably quick in the 1974 British 5000 series. Becoming the darling of the media, she achieved her results through consistency and took 5th place in the Championship. She even tried to qualify for the British Grand Prix but, despite creditable driving, she failed by a mere second. However, she did make her Grand Prix debut with March in the 1975 South African GP and finished a fortunate 6th in the Spanish GP but only scored half a point because the race was shortened by an accident.

As she always qualified near the back of the grid for the rest of the year Lella failed to secure a regular Grand Prix drive in 1976, although she made rare appearances in a March and a Brabham. Instead, she had to be content with Sports Car and Formula 5000 drives. After moderate success in Porsches, Lella once more hit success when she scored two wins in the 1979 WCM series – at Enna and Vallelunga – in her Osella. In 1981 she scored another outright win at Mugello and two superb second places at Monza and Enna.

A good Sports Car driver, and one of the most successful female drivers of recent years, Lella has proved herself to

Lella Lombardi.

be a serious racing driver rather than merely an attractive proposition for sponsors.

For The Record

First GP
1975 South Africa (March 741)

Best GP Result
6th 1975 Spain (March 751)

Lella made history by finishing 6th in the 1975 Spanish Grand Prix in her March.

Born in Birmingham on August 8, 1953, Nigel has shown great determination to succeed in motorsport. Racing karts from an early age, Nigel finished 3rd in the 1968 Junior Karting Championship finals in Milan, going on to win the Midland Kart Championship six times.

A qualified engineer, spending seven years with Lucas, Nigel found his job conflicting with his motor-racing interests which started seriously in 1976 when he entered Formula Ford. On a shoestring budget, Nigel turned professional in May 1977 – a month later breaking his neck in two places while racing! Despite this setback, the determined Brummie was racing within five weeks, winning the 1977 Brush Fusegear Formula Ford Title.

Without sponsorship, Nigel moved up to Formula 3 in 1978, selling his house and various other belongings in order to compete in a few races. At Silverstone his talent shone with a superb 2nd place behind Piquet from pole position.

A contract with the Unipart Formula 3 team in 1979 brought Nigel a win in the wet at Silverstone. However, an accident with de Cesaris at Oulton Park resulted in Nigel's car rolling and his damaging a

Nigel Mansell.

spinal column vertebra. Nigel had already impressed Lotus though, and, keeping the extent of his injuries a secret, turned up for their test session – winning a testing contract with the Formula 1 team for 1980, with the possibility of an occasional Grand Prix drive later in the season.

In the midst of the Lotus 88 controversy, Nigel's career hit a low point when he failed to qualify for the 1981 British Grand Prix. However, his performances in Belgium and Monaco earlier in the season showed his real potential.

Nigel's Grand Prix debut came during 1980, when, in Austria he drove a "development" Lotus. During the race a fuel leak gave him first and second degree burns, yet Nigel continued until his engine blew near the end – an impressive debut that led to a season-long contract for 1981.

Once the dispute over the revolutionary Lotus 88 seemed over, Nigel's precise but forceful driving came to the fore, allowing him to score an amazing 3rd place in Belgium. In Monaco the prospects looked even brighter, for, from a sensational 3rd on the grid he held 3rd in the race until Reutemann ran into the back of his car. A 6th in Spain followed. However, the Lotus's narrow side pods did not suit the fast circuits and so it was not until the North American races at the end of the season that Mansell shone again, collecting a 4th in Las Vegas.

Considered to be a top-line driver, Nigel will be hoping to score his first Grand Prix win during 1982....

For the Record

First GP
1980 Austria (Lotus 81B)

Best GP Result
3rd 1981 Belgium (Lotus 81)

Cool, cosmopolitan and charming, Jochen was born in Munich on September 30, 1946. Originally a merchant seaman, the pleasant German is still a keen sailor. His racing career began successfully with Alfa Romeo in 1968, and in 1969 he was signed up by Ford, finishing 2nd in the German Hillclimb Championship.

Excellent Formula 3 and Formula Vee performances in 1971 led March to sign-up Jochen for 1972 and he scored a fine win at the Eifelrennen Formula 2 round. Although finishing 2nd in the Springbok Sports Car series, the highlight of his year was clinching the European Touring Car Championship.

Signed-up by Surtees Formula 2 team in 1973, Jochen won at Hockenheim to finish 3rd in the series. As a result Surtees gave him his Grand Prix debut in Britain, and in Germany he finished 7th a mere second behind Fittipaldi.

Jochen Mass.

Jochen in an Arrows passes the abandoned cars of Laffite and Reutemann on his way to a reliable 2nd in the 1980 Spanish Grand Prix.

Leaving the Surtees' Grand Prix team midway through 1974, Jochen raced a works McLaren in the last two races of the year before begin signed-up to partner Fittipaldi in 1975. Once given competitive machinery, Jochen showed impressive confidence – finishing 3rd in Brazil. In Spain he scored his only Grand Prix win to date after a reliable drive, but only got half points as the race was shortened due to an accident. France saw the rapid German clearly outshine Fittipaldi, setting fastest lap on his way to 3rd place, a second behind Hunt whom he had pressurised for many laps. In the United States, however, the tables were turned and Jochen beat James to finish 3rd after a race-long battle.

Jochen proved inconsistent in 1976, although showing much early season promise in his McLaren. In Germany though, he gambled by racing on slicks on a wet track but, after two laps, his local knowledge proved correct and he found himself with an amazing 29-second lead before the race was stopped! In the restart he finished 3rd, as he had done previously in South Africa. Spectacular races in both Canada and Japan, combined with a tremendously successful Sports Car season with Porsche, assured him of retaining his place with McLaren. More often than not in the top six during 1977, Jochen failed to shine regularly although his performances in Belgium, Sweden,

Canada and Japan showed he was still a force to be reckoned with, and his Formula 2 victories showed he was still a winner.

1978 saw Jochen assume the role of team leader at ATS, but the team's failure to produce a competitive car ensured poor results. Bouncing back into form, following a testing accident at Silverstone, Jochen joined Arrows in 1979 and did a superb job with ageing equipment. His race at Monaco, where he moved up to 3rd before pitting, was tremendous. Once again in 1980, Jochen performed well at Monaco finishing 4th and in Spain he showed himself to be a pillar of reliability by finishing a distant 2nd. However, an accident during qualifying in Austria spoilt the rest of his season.

Left without a Grand Prix drive in 1981, Jochen drove Porsche Sports Cars – finishing 2nd at the Nurburgring. However, in 1982 he returns to the scene to lead the March Formula 1 team – keen to prove his ability and his standing as an established and experienced driver.

For The Record

First GP
1973 Britain (Surtees TS14A)

GP Win
1975 Spain (McLaren M23)

"Little Art", the son of a building contractor, was born on March 11 1943, near Lake Como, Italy, where he still lives today. Art raced and rallied an Alfa Romeo Spyder in 1963 before joining the works Fiat Abarth team to race a 1000 saloon in 1964, coming 2nd in the Italian Championship. After two years of National Service, Art raced Abarth Sports and Saloon cars from 1967 until joining the Ferrari Sports Car team in 1970. Racing a Ferrari 512S, Art was unfortunate to lose 2nd place at the Daytona 24-hours when he was overtaken just four minutes from the end!

In 1971, Art won the Interserie opener race at Imola in a Ferrari 312M and later ran an Abarth 2000SP in both Interserie and 2-litre rounds with success. 1972 saw Art winning both the Spa 1000Km and the Targa Florio in a Ferrari 312P; the latter against a full-strength Alfa Romeo team. Replacing an injured Regazzoni, Art came 6th in a Ferrari in his Formula 1 debut at the British Grand Prix, despite a stop to replace a punctured tyre. After another drive in Germany, Art had a full Formula 1 season with Ferrari in 1973, scoring two 4th places in Brazil and Argentina.

Moving to Iso Marlboro in 1974, Art contined to make moderate success, including a 6th place in South Africa. There followed a commendable 4th in Italy, after a cooked clutch at the line. After starting 1975 with Williams, Art moved on to concentrate on Sports Car racing – winning four races and coming 2nd in four others – before having a one-off drive in a Fittipaldi FD at Monza.

After driving for March, Williams and Shadow with little success, Art decided to build his own Formula 1 car on a limited budget during 1978/79. However in two seasons of racing, Art's best result in what can only be described as an uncompetitive car was an unclassified finish in the 1978 Swedish GP. Finding the cost of Formula 1 to be too great, Art moved to Formula 2 and continued to construct and race his own cars, but again with little success.

Depsite very successful Sports Car seasons with Alfa Romeo, notably 1975

Arturio Merzario.

and 1977, Art never really proved the potential shown in his first Grand Prix drives, although flashes of inspiration in 1976 showed that the talent was still there. He will always be remembered for his great courage and selflessness in rescuing Niki Lauda from his burning car at the Nurburgring in 1976.

For The Record

First GP
1972 Britain (Ferrari 312B2)

Best GP result
4th 1973 Brazil (Ferrari 312B2)
4th 1973 South Africa (Ferrari 312B2)
4th 1974 Italy (Iso-Marlboro FW03)

Art scored a commendable 4th in the 1974 Italian Grand Prix despite cooking the clutch of his Iso-Marlboro at the start.

Born on November 20 1948, this extrovert, ex-submarine radio officer, started racing Formula Vee in 1972. Moving on to Super-Vee the next year, Gunnar proved to be a wild, erratic driver, although he came 4th in a "one-off" Formula 2 drive at the Norisring. The young Swede thought that, as he had had little success in Continental Europe, it would be a good idea to come over to England to compete in Formula 3. After a moderate 1974 season, Gunnar, yet to win a major race, got a top-line works March Formula 3 drive for 1975. Beginning the season as he intended to continue, Gunnar won the first race at Thruxton. During the year he won at Thruxton again, at Snetterton and twice at Silverstone to win the BP Formula 3 title. Gunnar then became the sensation of the last few Formula Atlantic races of the series. In a Chevron B29 he won the wet race at Brands Hatch, lapping the Champion, Tony Brise, three times! The very next week, again at Brands Hatch, Gunnar pressurised Brise into a mistake and won impressively.

Gunnar was now much sought after in Formula 1 – Max Mosely of March thinking him to be a mixture of Lauda and Peterson – what a mixture! Eventually Gunnar signed for Lotus – making his debut in South Africa – but, although in Spain he came 3rd after a

Gunnar Nilsson.

brilliant drive in only his third Grand Prix, the season was on the whole disappointing despite good mid-season form in Germany and Austria promising much. Gunnar, with Quester, even tried his hand at Group 5 racing, winning the Osterreichring Six-Hours in a BMW. He followed this up with a win at the Nurburgring in 1977.

With the new Lotus 78 Gunnar proved that he could be really competitive: in Brazil he finished 5th,

Sadly Gunnar's only victory came in the 1977 Belgian Grand Prix when he drove a Lotus 78. During the race he displayed a talent the Formula 1 world has been so tragically denied seeing again.

despite two pit stops, and followed this up with another 5th in Spain. In Belgium it all came right. Gunnar qualified 3rd, the highest he had ever been on the grid, and held 2nd in the wet race until he had to pit for dry tyres. Within 20 laps, he had hauled his way up to 2nd again and, 20 laps from the end, he overtook Niki Lauda to score a magnificent victory, setting fastest lap on the way. Superb drives followed in Sweden where, after an early pit stop, he matched race-leader Andretti's pace. At Silverstone when, in the latter stages, he was permitted to pass his team-mate's ailing car and nearly caught Lauda in 2nd place. And at the Osterreichring where, in 21 laps, he passed Peterson, Reutemann, Depailler, Stuck, Lauda and Scheckter to take 3rd place before his engine blew.

After two years in Andretti's shadow, Gunnar decided that he had the qualifications to lead a team – so he signed up as Number One driver with the new Arrows team. Sadly Gunnar was never to sit in the car for, in December 1977, a pain that he had been troubled with all year, was diagnosed as a symptom of cancer. Despite being in constant pain, Gunnar refused pain-killing drugs in order to keep his mind alert to launch the Gunnar Nilsson Cancer Treatment Campaign which raised hundreds of thousands of pounds. Sadly, the amusing Swede, who had been tipped as a future World Champion, died on October 20, 1978.

For The Record

First GP
1976 South Africa (Lotus 77)

GP win
1977 Belgium (Lotus 78)

Keith Jack Oliver was born on August 14, 1942. His racing career began when he bought an 800cc Mini and entered a few hillclimb and club meetings. Success first came when Jackie won a number of races during 1962 in a Marcos, and in 1963 he had a competitive season when he switched to driving a Lotus Elan. Seven wins in nine starts in his Ford Mustang, during 1966, led to his being made runner-up in the Grovewood Award of that year. Seen as one of the most promising British newcomers, Jackie had signed a three-year contract with Lotus by the beginning of 1967, and scored two Formula 2 victories before the year was out.

His Grand Prix debut came in 1968 with Lotus and, in Belgium, he scored his first points for 5th place. A "veteran" of Brands Hatch since his earlier racing days he used all his track knowledge to qualify 2nd and lead the British Grand Prix from the start. This was only his fifth Grand Prix and he led for three laps before team-mate Hill passed him, but recaptured the lead when Graham retired. Lapping consistently and looking set for victory, Jackie retired at half-distance. He was, however, rewarded for his efforts by a 3rd place in Mexico.

In 1969 he switched to driving for BRM, but the car proved hopelessly

Jackie Oliver.

uncompetitive and unreliable although Jackie picked up a 6th in Mexico. This year also saw him win at Sebring and Le Mans with Ickx, in a Ford GT40, proving his adaptability as a driver.

In 1970 the BRM proved more competitive as Jackie diced for 3rd place in South Africa, Holland and Britain before retiring, but kept going in Austria to pick up a 5th place. His best showing

One of Jackie's best results came when he drove his Shadow to 3rd place in the wet 1973 Canadian Grand Prix at the end of his last complete Formula 1 season.

of the year, however, came at Monza where he led the slipstreaming pack across the line no less than eight times before his engine blew. Occasional Formula 1 drives with McLaren followed in 1971, but his best results were achieved in Porsche Sports Cars with Rodriguez, and in Can-Am towards the end of the year.

In 1972 Jackie had a one-off Grand Prix drive at Brands Hatch for BRM, and in 1973 he completed a full season with Shadow, scoring a tremendous 3rd in the wet Canadian event that he had led for a handful of laps. The next year he was relegated to the Shadow Can-Am team, but dominated the Championship, winning four of the five races.

Concentrating on managing the business side of Shadow racing, Jackie kept his hand in by competing in Formula 5000 in the United States during 1975 and 1976. So, when he was offered a Formula 1 drive in the Race of Champions and in the Swedish Grand Prix with the team in 1977, he proved to be impressive for a man without a regular GP drive, finishing 5th at the Brands Hatch event.

Leaving Shadow at the end of the year, he became a founding member of the Arrows outfit – the 'O' in ArrOws standing for Oliver. Although never totally fulfilling his potential, Jackie showed flashes of brilliance, notably at Brands Hatch in 1968 and at Monza in 1970 where he led until retiring.

For The Record

First GP
1968 Monaco (Lotus 49)

Best GP Result
3rd 1968 Mexico (Lotus 49)
3rd 1973 Canada (Shadow DN1)

The son of a wealthy textile family, Brazilian Carlos Pace was born on October 6, 1944. He started racing a modified Renault Dauphine at 18, before becoming three-times Brazilian Champion (1967, 1968 and 1969) driving an Alfa Romeo T33.

Carlos arrived in Europe in 1969 amid tales of his racing potential being as good as fellow Brazilian Emerson Fittipaldi. After a successful Formula 3 season in 1970, in which he took the Forward Trust Championship, he moved up to compete in a March Formula 2 car, entered by Frank Williams, the following year – scoring an impressive win at Imola. Staying with Frank WIlliams for 1972, Carlos had his first season in Formula 1. He came 6th in Spain and 5th in Belgium in an uncompetitive car, impressing everyone with his smooth handling: people began to believe the stories of his prowess emanating from Brazil ....

Carlos Pace.

Carlos's only Grand Prix win came when he drove a Brabham in front of his emotional Brazilian home crowd in 1975.

Changing teams to Surtees for 1973, Carlos had a string of three brilliant drives, starting in Holland, where he was 3rd, in the early laps until the front tyres overheated. In Germany Carlos smashed the lap record by 2.2 seconds on his way to a fighting 4th place before, two weeks later, coming 3rd in Austria, again breaking the lap record.

Still with Surtees in 1974, Carlos, even though he came 4th in Brazil, became disillusioned and left the team mid-season to drive for Brabham for the rest of the year. After great races in Austria and Italy, Carlos finished the year with a good 2nd place and fastest lap at Watkins Glen.

1975 saw Carlos' only Grand Prix victory – an emotional win in front of his home, Sao Paulo, crowd – after another good showing in Argentina. He scored his first pole position, and a 4th place, in South Africa five weeks later. In Spain, he was just about to take Stommelen for the lead when Stommelen crashed, taking Carlos with him. At Monaco he gambled on dry tyres in a wet race, and still came 3rd. In another wet race, at Silverstone, Carlos led for the first thirteen laps and finally finished 2nd.

Unfortunately, in 1976 Carlos was let down by an over-weight, unreliable car and engine, although he still had good drives in France and Germany. He started the 1977 season well in Argentina with a 2nd place, which could have been a 1st place until he had to drop back feeling faint due to lack of fresh air. However, after another two drives in the Brabham, sadly, Carlos was killed in a light aeroplane crash in Brazil. The accident happened at a stage in Carlos' career when he had proven himself as top-line driver ready for greater things, perhaps even a crack at the World Championship ... The approachable Brazilian was mourned by a nation to whom he had become as much of an idol as Emerson Fittipaldi.

For The Record

First GP
1972 South Africa (March 711)

GP win
1975 Brazil (Brabham BT44B)

Born on April 17, 1954, Riccardo Patrese's reputation is considerably blacker than it should be. The Italian began his career as twice World Karting Champion (1973 and 1974) which was a firm basis from which to move up the motor racing ladder. First in Formula Italia, where he was narrowly defeated by Giacomelli in the 1975 Championship – and then into Formula 3 – winning both 1976 Italian and European Championships, Riccardo had proved that he had the credentials needed to reach the top.

Moving swiftly through Formula 2, he made an impressive Grand Prix debut at Monaco in 1977; especially impressive considering his only previous Formula 1

Riccardo Patrese.

Riccardo's moment of glory came when he qualified on pole position at Long Beach in 1981, and went on to lead the race from Reutemann until forced to drop back with fuel feed problems in his Arrows car.

experience was a brief Paul Ricard test session. Showing skill and confidence, Riccardo was rewarded with a 6th in Japan.

Joining the brand new Arrows team in 1978, Riccardo's year began promisingly with a remarkable drive to 1st place in South Africa and, after another good drive in Belgium, finishing a fine 2nd in Sweden, despite pressure from an on-form Peterson. However, blamed for the crash which proved fatal for Peterson at Monza, Riccardo's driving suffered throughout 1979.

The South American races in 1980 proved mildly encouraging, and paved the way for a steady drive at Long Beach which resulted in a 2nd place as the field disintegrated. A year later, at the same track, Riccardo notched up his first pole position and led until forced to drop back with fuel feed problems.

Proving Long Beach wasn't just a flash in the pan, he finished a superb 3rd in Brazil and a competitive 2nd in San Marino. Unfortunately, after Monaco, the fortunes of the team waned and so he will have to wait for another opportunity to score his first Grand Prix win. By joining Brabham for 1982, alongside World Champion Nelson Piquet, Riccardo has a chance to prove his ability beyond doubt.

For The Record

First GP
1977 Monaco (Shadow DN8)

Best GP Result
2nd 1978 Sweden (Arrows FA1)
2nd 1980 Long Beach (Arrows A3)
2nd 1981 San Marino (Arrows A3)

The son of a well-known French surgeon, Henri was born on September 25, 1942, and started his motor racing career at 23 years of age in a Lotus 7. In 1966 he became a member of the Matra Formula 3 team, scoring two victories. By the following year he was generally considered to be the fastest European F3 driver, for he won nine times and became French Formula 3 Champion.

1968 saw Henri graduate to Formula 2 with Matra, but, despite ending the season well with a win at Albi and finishing runner-up in the European Championship, his expected move to Formula 1 did not come about because Matra handed over their Grand Prix operation to Ken Tyrrell. Instead, Henri had to be content with Formula 2 and Sports Cars for another year, before moving into Grand Prix racing with Matra in 1970. The Matras proved reliable, but not particularly fast – a perfect recipe for a 3rd place at Monaco! A 5th in France, 6th in Belgium and Germany combined to produce the Frenchman's most successful Formula 1 season.

Moving to Frank Williams' low-budget March team in 1971, Henri finished 2nd in the non-Championship Argentine Grand Prix and did an extremely good job to finish 4th in Britain and 6th in Austria. Wins at the Mallory Park Formula 2 round and the BOAC 1000Km showed Henri's adaptability and all-round racing skill.

Henri Pescarolo.

Henri had the misfortune to join particular Formula 1 teams when their fortunes were low. In 1974 he drove for BRM and in 1976 he raced a private Surtees, but never proved competitive. Instead, he concentrated on Sports Cars, winning Le Mans three years running from 1972 to 1974 in a Matra-Simca. His highly successful Sports Car career with Matra was followed by seasons with Alfa Romeo, Renault, Porsche and Rondeau, his most recent success being a 2nd at Watkins Glen in a Lancia with de Cesaris in 1981.

Henri did an extremely good job to finish 4th at the 1971 British Grand Prix in Frank Williams' under-financed March.

The bearded Frenchman has never really been considered a top-line Grand Prix driver, even though he has had extensive Formula 1 and Sports Car experience. It is too late for him to return to Formula 1 now, but he may well win for a fourth time at Le Mans in the future!

For The Record

First GP
1970 Spain (Matra-Simca MS120)

Best GP Result
3rd 1970 Monaco (Matra-Simca MS120)

The tall, blond Swede was born on February 14, 1944, the son of a baker-cum-amateur-engineer in Orebro, Sweden. When he was 18 his father built him a kart and between 1963 and 1966 he won no less than five Swedish Kart Championships – also finishing well in the 1966 World Championship.

Having had the occasional Formula 3 race in a homemade car during 1966, Ronnie bought a Brabham and soon produced some promising drives, winning the 1968 Swedish Championship when he switched to driving a Tecno. Choosing a Tecno again in 1969, Ronnie won seven successive Formula 3 races including the prestigious Monaco round. Despite crashing badly at Montlhery, March still offered the dashing Swede a three-year contract while he was in hospital!

Ronnie did a fine job for March by qualifying on his Grand Prix debut at Monaco and then nearly finishing in the points with a drive to 7th place! In Formula 2 he led the March team, having had an excellent drive at Rouen and eventually finishing 4th in the Championship.

For 1971 Ronnie had the new March 711 and with it established himself as a topline Formula 1 driver. In a mature, polished performance he came 2nd at Monaco, to score his first World Championship points. Another 2nd in Britain, was followed by near-victory in Italy where he was beaten to the line by 1/1000th sec. having led much of the race. At the wet Canadian Grand Prix he led Stewart, but eventually succumbed to pressure and had to be content with 2nd, creditably finishing runner-up in the World Championship in only his first full season! In Formula 2, in his March, Ronnie was Champion with four wins to his credit – three of them consecutively.

1972, however, proved to be disastrous. With the experimental March being uncompetitive and his regular car unreliable, Ronnie's best result was a 3rd in Germany behind the two Ferraris. Not satisfied with a 2nd at the non-Championship Brazilian Grand Prix and a win in the Thruxton Formula 2 round,

Ronnie Peterson.

Ronnie moved to Lotus for 1973.

Incredibly, Ronnie set nine pole positions during 1973 and in doing so regularly outqualified Fittipaldi the World Champion who was his team leader. The "SuperSwede's" desire to win had to wait until France for fulfilment, despite fine early season performances. In Austria he led before waving his team-mate past; only to inherit the lead when Emerson retired. In Italy and the United States, Ronnie dominated the race from pole position.

Because he was unlucky not to have won more races, Ronnie's fans began to tip him to take over the retired Stewart's mantle of World Champion in 1974. But it was not to be, for, although fearless speed and determination brought success in Monaco, France and Italy – in an outdated Lotus 72 – his superb racing prowess on vastly different kinds of circuit failed to secure that elusive title.

Staying with Lotus a year too long, in hindsight, Ronnie moved down the grid in 1975, although he put up an amazing performance at Monaco to push the ageing Lotus into 2nd place before a pit stop dropped him to 4th. Splitting from Lotus after the 1976 Brazilian Grand Prix, Ronnie rejoined March who provided a fast but fragile

Incredibly, during 1973, Ronnie's superb car control combined with the Lotus 72 chassis put him on pole position nine times and scored him four fine wins.

car. Having led from pole in Austria and Holland, Ronnie finally won again in Italy before moving to Tyrrell for 1977.

A disappointing 1977 season with the unreliable Tyrrell 6-wheelers yielded only a 3rd in Belgium and so it was, with a lessened reputation, that he rejoined Lotus in 1978 as Andretti's team-mate. A last lap win over Depailler in South Africa brought him back onto the victory trail. In Belgium, a superb drive through the field, after a poor start, to finish 2nd, gave Lotus the first of four 1-2 victories for 1978: the others being in Spain, France and Holland. In Austria, though, it was Ronnie who gave an impressive demonstration by leading practically all the way in the wet race, after Andretti had spun out on the first lap.

A month later, on September 11, 1978, the "SuperSwede" was dead – tragically killed as the result of a start-line accident at Monza: ironically the track where he had won no less than three Grands Prix.

Ronnie was a driver of immense natural talent who never gave up however far down the lap charts his car placed him – a characteristic that brought him much well-deserved acclaim.

For The Record

First GP
1970 Monaco (March 701)

GP Wins
1973 France (Lotus 72)
1973 Austria (Lotus 72)
1973 Italy (Lotus 72)
1973 United States (Lotus 72)
1974 Monaco (Lotus 72)
1974 France (Lotus 72)
1974 Italy (Lotus 72)
1976 Italy (March 761)
1978 South Africa (Lotus 78)
1978 Austria (Lotus 79)

'A very good race driver, rather in the mould of Lauda' is how Gordon Murray, the Brabham designer, summed up the talent of this Brazilian, who was born on August 17, 1952. Nelson's real name is Souto Maier but, so that his family would not know about his racing exploits, he used the pseudonym 'Piquet'. His racing career began when, forsaking tennis, he took up Karting in 1970. In 1972 he won the Brazilian Sports Car Championship and moved up to Super Vee in 1974.

After winning the 1976 Super Vee title he travelled to Europe to compete in Formula 3 in 1977, following advice from Emerson Fittipaldi. That year brought him success as he came 3rd in the European Championship. He won the BP Formula 3 Championship in 1978, and, after some outings in the Ensign Formula 1 car at the end of the year, was invited to partner Niki Lauda in the Brabham team in 1979. Nelson often outqualified his double World Champion team leader, but unreliability of his cars ruined some otherwise good drives.

The sudden retirement of Niki Lauda, before the end of the 1979 season, meant that Piquet became Brabham team leader. The appearance of the new Brabham BT49 showed the

Nelson Piquet.

potential of the Brazilian as he put the car on the front row of the grid at Watkins Glen. In 1980, he won three Grands Prix and nearly pipped Alan Jones to becoming World Champion, but had to be satisfied with the consolation of winning the BMW Pro-Car Championship.

Nelson started 1981 well in the new Brabham with hydro-pneumatic

A superb driver with great natural ability, Nelson won the 1981 World Championship with Brabham in only his third full Grand Prix season!

suspension, winning in Argentina – where he was untouchable – and San Marino. A series of mid-season accidents under pressure – though not all Nelson's own fault – allowed Reutemann to streak away into the Championship lead. However, a win in Germany, a 3rd in Austria and a 2nd in Holland put Nelson level on points with the Argentinian. In Italy Nelson's engine blew within sight of the line, handing his 3rd place to arch-rival Reutemann, although a 5th in Canada put Nelson one point behind Reutemann with one round to go – in Las Vegas. Suffering considerable pain from strained neck muscles, Nelson, in a drive of great stamina, finished a worthy 5th in a performance that earned him the 1981 World Championship.

A driver of superb natural ability, it has been suggested that Nelson has yet to reach his peak in his motor racing career. When he does he may well be near-unbeatable!

For The Record

First GP
1978 German (Ensign N177)

GP Wins
1980 United States, West
       (Brabham BT49)
1980 Holland (Brabham BT49)
1980 Italy (Brabham BT49)
1981 Argentina (Brabham BT49C)
1981 San Marino (Brabham BT49C)
1981 Germany (Brabham BT49C)

World Champion
1981 (Brabham)

Born on March 26, 1952, this quiet, unassuming Frenchman first found interest in motor-racing when he worked as a mechanic for his cousin. Enthusiastic, he enrolled at a racing school and won a scholarship, which included a works Formula Renault drive in 1973. Despite a poor year he made amends by later going on to win both the French and European Formula Renault titles.

Moving straight into Formula 2 for the 1977 season, he strung together a number of impressive drives before rounding off the year with a dominant win at Estoril. Proving his potential by winning the Monaco Formula 3 race, Didier was invited to join the Tyrrell Grand Prix team in 1978. Quickly settling into the demands of Formula 1 racing he scored his first point in Brazil for 6th place in only his second race! Reliable drives followed, a habit that obviously aided the young Frenchman when he tackled – and won – the Le Mans 24-hour race in a Renault-Alpine!

Although the 1979 season yielded two 3rd places – at Zolder and Watkins Glen – it was not until Didier joined Ligier in 1980 that his talent blossomed. Immediately proving to be the equal of established team leader Laffite, he

Didier Pironi.

proved unbeatable in Belgium – scoring a splendid start-to-finish victory. At Monaco, from pole position, he showed his maturity by holding off a most determined attack by Jones whilst leading, until crashing when his car jumped out of gear. At Brands Hatch wheel and tyre trouble spoilt what would

Didier's Turbo Ferrari burns rubber as it accelerates hard at Silverstone during 1981.

have been an unchallenged win, for, having set pole position, Didier was forced to pit before rejoining in 21st place. Destroying the lap record, he had aggressively moved up through the field to 4th place before finally retiring. In Canada, he once again broke the lap record and won the race on the road, but was classified 3rd due to a one minute penalty for a jumped start. During a year in which he proved to be a match for anyone when his equipment was right, Didier deserved more than a single win.

Joining Ferrari in 1981 Didier showed the potential of the new turbo engine by leading both the San Marino and the Belgian races. His determination to win was shown by his breathtaking start at Monza where he moved from 8th on the grid to 2nd at the end of the first lap! With the arrival of a new Ferrari chassis, Didier – a driver of immense talent – could well earn a regular place on the top of the rostrum during 1982.

For The Record

First GP
1978 Argentina (Tyrrell 008)

GP Win
1980 Belgium (Ligier JS11/15)

Born on February 24, 1955, this gifted, agreeable Frenchman nearly took up professional football, rather than motor racing! Alain seems intent on dominating every formula of racing he enters; a trend that began when he won twelve of the thirteen races in the 1976 French Formula Renault Championship, and, of course, the title. The next year he was victorious in winning the European Formula Renault title.

1978 saw Alain not only share victory in the French Formula 3 series, but also score his first European Formula 3 victory, at Jarama. Seven more victories followed in 1979 when Alain swept all before him. With over double the points of the second placed man in the Championship, and a victory at the prestigious Monaco event under his belt, Alain was offered a winter test at Paul Ricard with the McLaren Formula 1 team – his methodical approach earning him a place alongside Watson in 1980.

An exceptional debut in Argentina gave Alain his first Championship point and his impressive maturity was to earn him a 5th place in Brazil two weeks later. A broken wrist due to a practice accident in South Africa, however, delayed the young man's progress. Although only pisking up two 6th places in the remainder of that year, Alain had shown

Alain Prost.

his potential by outqualifying his team leader for much of the season. Renault snapped him up for 1981 when Jabouille moved to Ligier.

A 3rd in Argentina gave some indication of what was to come, but the rest of the first half of the season was spoilt by mechanical failures and

Alain proved to be the sensation of 1981, scoring excellent victories in France, Holland and Italy driving a Renault Turbo.

mistakes by other drivers. That was until France, where the race was split into two halves because of rain. 2nd in part one and 1st in part two was enough for overall victory,although Alain could not have been totally happy with the way he achieved his win.

Total domination was what he wanted and this he had in Britain, Germany and Austria until mechanical ailments intervened. However, from pole position in Holland Alain won again, beating off a determined challenge from Jones and showing that, not only did he have a shrewd tactical sense, but a great fighting spirit. Leading from start to finish, Alain was victorious in Italy as well. Many put these successes down to the power of the Renault Turbo on fast circuits, but these doubters were proved wrong when Alain turned in two tremendous performances on the slow street circuits of North America, leading in Canada and finishing 2nd, after a pit stop, in Las Vegas.

Sure to be a strong contender for the 1982 World Championship, Alain must hope for mechanical reliability throughout the season.

For The Record

First GP
1980 Argentina (McLaren M29B)

GP Wins
1981 France (Renault RE30)
1981 Holland (Renault RE30)
1981 Italy (Renault RE30)

Tom – the quiet, shy son of a policeman – was born on June 11, 1949. His career began when he won a Formula Ford car in a competition. Racing in England, the young Welshman used the name 'Tom' in preference to his less easily pronounced Welsh name and soon found success. In 1971 he was one of the men to beat in Formula Super Vee, and he dominated the F100 series. The next year he showed good early season form before a bad practice accident at Monaco.

In 1973 he raced both Formula Atlantic and Formula 2, finishing 2nd to Schenken at the Norisring Formula 2 round. This was enough to earn him the major Grovewood Motor Racing Award and keep him in Formula 2 until 1974. Running a Chevron at the start of the year, Tom qualified on pole in Austria and had his first Formula 1 drive in the Token at the Silverstone International Trophy, making his Grand Prix debut in Belgium a month later.

Driving a March in the Monaco Formula 3 race, Tom won his heat and final convincingly. He impressed the Shadow team enough for them to give him a drive for the remainder of the year; Tom scoring his first World Championship point in Germany after a sensible drive.

Tom Pryce.

In 1975, the new Shadow DN5 immediately pushed Tom further up the grid, culminating in his first and only pole position in the British Grand Prix where he led for a time until crashing in the wet. Two weeks later in Germany Tom had driven the car into 2nd place before the intense discomfort of a fuel leak in his cockpit forced him to drop back to 4th. Later, at the wet Osterreichring, Tom's

Tom seemed certain to notch up a 2nd place in the 1976 Brazilian Grand Prix until locking brakes and worn tyres on his Shadow dropped him into the clutches of Depailler.

car control showed with a fine 3rd place, followed by a 6th after a consistent drive in Italy. Although Grand Prix success eluded him in 1975, Tom had won the non-Championship Race of Champions at Brands Hatch earlier in the year. A victory destined to be his only Formula 1 win....

During 1976, after a good drive to 3rd place in Brazil, Tom repeatedly outqualified his team-mate Jarier, and came 4th in Britain and Holland. Holding an excellent 2nd place in Japan for seven laps ultimately came to nothing because of engine failure. Again, in 1977, in Brazil Tom was just seven laps away from finishing 2nd when his engine blew. After these superb drives, it was even more saddening to hear of Tom's death through no fault of his own, or of his car. During the South African Grand Prix, a young marshal – rushing to douse flames from Zorzi's abandoned car – ran into the path of Tom's speeding Shadow DN8, and the Welsh star was killed instantly when struck by the marshal's fire-extinguisher. The motor racing world had lost one of its most unassuming and talented drivers. Tom met his death before he had scored that Grand Prix win which he so deserved....

For The Record

First GP
1974 Belgian (Token RJ)

Best GP Result
3rd 1975 Austria (Shadow DN5)
3rd 1976 Brazil (Shadow DN5)

This wealthy Mexican was born on February 5, 1956. In 1971 he began racing on dirt ovals in saloon cars. Proving successful, Hector moved to America to compete in a number of endurance races. In 1974 he travelled to Europe to compete in Formula Atlantic and some Sports Car events, including Le Mans. In 1975 he turned to European Formula 2 and, after coming 4th in two early season races, crossed the Atlantic again to compete in some Canadian Formula Atlantic events, where he stayed for the 1976 season.

In 1977, Hector made his first tentative steps in Formula 1 racing with the Hesketh team. He had only one uninspiring race, qualifying last on the grid and retiring after 20 laps. After this experience Hector formed his own team for 1978, by purchasing ex-works Lotus 78s. It was a dismal season of very low grid positions and mechanical problems. However, in the German Grand Prix he showed more gusto than before, finishing 6th.

For the 1979 season, he purchased some ex-works Lotus 79s. At first he had problems with learning the smooth driving technique required with the new Lotus, but he had promising drives at Long Beach, Zolder and Zandvoort. From the Italian Grand Prix onwards

Hector Rebaque.

Hector took on the role of driver-constructor with the Rebaque HR100 built by Penske, which was immaculately prepared, but uncompetitive.

At the end of 1979 the team issued a statement saying that Goodyear had not produced the promised competitive qualifying and race tyres and, therefore, the team could not fulfil its responsibility to sponsors and supporters. Also the

Undoubtedly Hector was at his most inspired during the 1981 Argentine Grand Prix, for he pushed his Brabham into a comfortable 2nd place until forced to retire.

team felt that the official bodies had not offered worthwhile assistance and therefore the team was forced reluctantly, to disband. However, with sponsorship, Hector joined the Brabham team midway through 1980. Gradually his qualifying times improved, earning him a 6th place in Canada.

Maturing, Hector drove his best ever race in Argentina 1981, where he moved his Brabham up to 2nd before a mechanical breakage intervened. Reward for this performance came in San Marino, where Hector finished 4th. In France Hector showed great determination in clawing his way up to 6th and in Britain he finished 5th despite two pit stops! Excellent 4ths in Germany and Holland followed, showing that Gordon Murray, the Brabham designer, was right when he said: 'for the experience he's had and the limited races, and the break in his career which is always difficult to come back from, he's pretty good.'

For The Record

First GP
1977 Germany (Hesketh 308E)

Best GP Results
4th 1981 San Marino (Brabham BT49C)
4th 1981 Germany (Brabham BT49C)
4th 1981 Holland (Brabham BT49C)

This ever-enthusiastic Lancastrian and former mop salesman was born on March 9, 1937 and had his first taste of motor racing in 1959 with a Morris Minor! Up until 1965 he competed in various cars in club events, but after a successful 1965 season in an E-type Jaguar he decided to start racing seriously in a Group 7 Lola.

Impressive in Formula 2 and in Endurance Racing, Brian was engaged on a race-to-race basis with the Cooper Formula 1 team during 1968, scoring a fortunate 3rd place in Spain where only five cars finished! However, in Belgium he crashed and broke his arm when the suspension of his car collapsed.

Although very successful with Ford, Porsche and Chevron Sports Cars, Brian's attempts to return to the Formula 1 scene seemed doomed to failure as he was involved in both the abortive 1969 Cosworth and the 1970 de Tomaso projects. Disappointed, he retired at the end of 1970 and emigrated to South Africa.

Brian Redman.

Tempted to return by a one-off drive in the 1971 South African Grand Prix, Brian finished 7th in the Surtees and went on to become the early pacesetter in Formula 5000 and Interserie before a fiery accident at the Targa Florio forced

Deputising for Revson at Team McLaren, Brian drove his M19A skilfully at Monaco in 1972 to finish 5th.

him to spend nearly three months away from the tracks.

In 1972 Brian was asked to drive in selected Grands Prix for McLaren when Revson was otherwise committed. He did an admirable job, driving with determination to finish 5th in both Monaco and Germany, 9th in France after a pit stop, and a superb 2nd in the non-Championship Rothmans' "50,000" race at Brands Hatch.

A successful 1972 European Formula 5000 season was followed by five wins in the American F5000 series the following year in which he eventually finished runner-up to Scheckter. An unprecedented domination of the United States Formula 5000 scene resulted in Brian's winning the title for three consecutive years – 1974, 1975 and 1976. These performances, combined with Sports Car success with Ferrari and BMW, resulted in Brian's competing in three early 1974 European Grands Prix for Shadow, though a 7th in Spain proved to be his best result.

With Formula 5000 disbanding, Brian hoped to compete in Can-Am during 1977, but during practice for the first round at St. Jovite his car flipped over at high speed. Recovery was a long process, for Brian had sustained a broken neck and many other serious injuries. Indeed, many thought he would never race again, but doubters were proved wrong when on his comeback drive he won the 1978 Sebring 12-hours. Brian's career in Sports Cars blossomed again when he won the 1981 IMSA Championship with six superb wins, before announcing his retirement in January 1982. However, he plans to remain in the United States where he has lived since late 1981, to work for Ford Special Vehicle Operations.

Brian's tremendous victories in Sports Cars, and especially in Formula 5000, have shown that a successful Formula 1 career would undoubtedly have followed if he had been able to secure regular drives.

For The Record

First GP
1968 South Africa (Cooper T81B-Maserati)

Best GP Result
3rd 1968 Spain (Cooper T86B-BRM)

Gianclaudio Regazzoni, better known as 'Clay', was born on September 5, 1939, in Lugano, Switzerland. Clay began hillclimbing relatively late in life, but, after a driving course at the Swiss Racing School, Silvio Moser encouraged Clay to move on to Formula 3, resulting in a win at Jarama in 1967 driving a Tecno. His unsuccessful 1968 season saw many crashes – the one at Zandvoort sadly involving, and killing, Chris Lambert.

Clay, however, attracted the attention of the Ferrari Formula 2 team and was signed-up for 1969 – but the cars were totally uncompetitive. 1970 saw the European Formula 2 title come Clay's way after three wins and some impressive drives in non-Championship Formula 2 races. A skilful 4th place in his Grand Prix debut, preceded a victory in a Ferrari in front of the delighted Italian crowds at Monza. Incredibly, Clay came 3rd in the World Championship even though he had only competed in eight of the thirteen races in the series. He qualified well each time and gained his first pole position in Mexico.

1971 and 1972 were not such successful years, due to unreliable cars and an accident prone Regazzoni, his

Clay Regazzoni.

only successes coming in the Ferrari 312P Sports Car. Switching to BRM in 1973, Clay immediately took pole position in the season's first race in Argentina. However, the rest of his lacklustre year was notable only for a fiery accident in South Africa, from which he

Clay drove his Ensign into 4th place at Long Beach in 1980 before an appalling accident ended his racing career.

was rescued by a courageous Hailwood.

Clay, noticeably matured and consistent, returned to Ferrari in 1974 with his ex-BRM team-mate Niki Lauda. Despite only recording one win – in Germany – Clay went into the final round at Watkins Glen on level points with Fittipaldi, only to lose the title by 3 points when he retired and Emerson finished 4th!

The last two races of the 1975 season, when he had to play a somewhat reluctant second fiddle to Lauda, highlighted the two approaches of Clay well. In Italy, the "dominant" Clay led all the way, setting the fastest lap. In the United States, the "controversial" Clay was black-flagged for badly baulking Fittipaldi, who was chasing Lauda, and was withdrawn by Ferrari as a protest to the organiser!

Winning at Long Beach in 1976 was probably Clay's greatest triumph but, by the end of the year, he had found disfavour in the Ferrari camp, and left for Ensign. Here, chiefly due to engine problems, he was unable to show his true form. A bad 1978 season with Shadow, including five non-qualifications, led most people to assume that Clay was no longer his former competitive self.

1979 showed that this was definitely not the case as Clay proved that given the tools he could finish the job. Williams supplied the FW07 and Clay, after a sensational performance at Monaco, won a splendid victory at Silverstone, and, two weeks later, came home 2nd in Germany.

Going back to Ensign for 1980, Clay started what he intended to be his last season before retirement. At Long Beach Clay had worked the car up into 4th place when tragedy struck. Approaching a hairpin at the end of a 170mph straight, Clay's car had complete brake failure and he suffered one of the most severe crashes in Grand Prix history, one that cost Clay the use of his legs and ended the career of one of the sport's greatest characters.

For The Record

First GP
1970 Holland (Ferrari 312B)

GP Wins
1970 Italy (Ferrari 312B)
1974 Germany (Ferrari 312B3)
1975 Italy (Ferrari 312T)
1976 United States, West (Ferrari 312T)
1979 Britain (Williams FW07)

Sometimes unbeatable, sometimes an also-ran, this introverted Argentinian was born on April 12, 1942. Carlos' career began after a test drive for Fiat in 1965 and, by 1968, he had become a well-known figure in Argentinian racing having won the National Touring Car Championship for three consecutive years. In the Temporada as well as in the European Formula 2 series, he reaped little reward until 1971 when he finished runner-up to Peterson in the European Championship – a result of consistency, for he scored no outright wins!

Signed-up by the Brabham Formula 1 team for 1972, Carlos became a national hero when he stunned the Grand Prix establishment by securing pole position on his Grand Prix debut in front of his home crowd. However, this early pace did not continue and it was not until the Canadian event, late in the year, that he scored his first points by finishing 4th.

Ending 1973 with a fine 3rd place at Watkins Glen, Carlos started the 1974 season confidently. Indeed, in Argentina he took the lead on the third lap and pulled away from the rest of the field with

Carlos Reutemann.

apparent ease until sidelined for the want of a pint of petrol on the last lap! After another good outing in Brazil, Carlos passed Lauda in the South African race to score the first of three dominant wins that season, although his title hopes were dashed by mid-season retirements.

The combined reliability and speed of his Williams during 1981 helped Carlos to have his best crack at the World Title.

Handling problems struck his Brabham during 1975 whilst he was leading in the Argentinian, Brazilian and Swedish Grands Prix but, in Germany, he scored an unexpected win. After a season of retirements in 1976, Carlos became disillusioned and left Brabham after five seasons to join Ferrari.

Although the year started well for the Argentinian with a win in Brazil, his performances never really matched those of Lauda, but consistent placings pushed him up the World Championship order. Unfortunately for Carlos, his shot at the Championship as leader of the Ferrari team in 1978 came in the year of Andretti's domination, and, despite his four victories, he was otherwise only able to score two 2nd and three 3rd places.

Ironically, he left Ferrari, who were destined to win the 1979 title, to join the Lotus team – who had one of their worst years ever. Even so, he was the only driver even remotely able to worry the Ligiers in South America, qualified an excellent 2nd at Long Beach, and drove gritty races in Spain, Belgium and Monaco.

Switching to Williams in 1980, Carlos began, in Belgium, an amazing series of **fifteen** consecutive finishes in the points which ended with a win in the 1981 Belgian Grand Prix. This incredible consistency seemed, from the start, to mark 1981 as Carlos' year, for, after the British event, he had a seemingly unassailable **seventeen point lead** in the World Championship. However, after the British GP his race performances lacked the sparkle and confidence they had earlier in the season... As a result, he lost the Championship by a single, frustrating point to Piquet.

Carlos, who had been a major force in Grand Prix racing for ten seasons, stayed with Williams for the 1982 season but announced his retirement from the sport after the first two Grands Prix.

For The Record

First GP
1972 Argentina (Brabham BT34)

GP Wins
1974 South Africa (Brabham BT44)
1974 Austria (Brabham BT44)
1974 United States (Brabham BT44)
1975 Germany (Brabham BT44B)
1977 Brazil (Ferrari 312T2)
1978 Brazil (Ferrari 312T2)
1978 United States, West (Ferrari 312T3)
1978 Britain (Ferrari 312T3)
1978 United States, East (Ferrari 312T3)
1980 Monaco (Williams FW07B)
1981 Brazil (Williams FW07C)
1981 Belgium (Williams FW07C)

Peter, born on February 27, 1939, was the son of one of the founders of the Revlon Cosmetics Empire, though not heir to their fortunes. Having watched SCCA Sports Car racing in Hawaii he decided to celebrate his 21st birthday by racing his Morgan. After racing Formula Junior in 1961-2, Peter arrived in Europe in 1963; winning at Roskilde in his FJ Cooper and having his first Formula 1 drive at the Oulton Park Gold Cup in a Parnell-entered Lotus 24.

Running his own Lotus in a few 1964 Grands Prix Peter gained little more than experience, his best result being 13th in Italy. With no Formula 1 drive in 1965, Peter raced Formula 3 and occasionally Formula 2, winning the Monaco Formula 3 race. Impressive drives in a Ford GT40 and a McLaren Can-Am car led to Goodyear arranging a drive at Indianapolis in Jack Brabham's second car during 1969. From 33rd on the grid, he finished a fine 5th, winning at the Indianapolis Raceway Park a few weeks later in the same car.

2nd in the 1970 Sebring 12-hours race, with actor Steve McQueen, Peter also had some encouraging Can-Am races, winning the Championship the next year in great style with five wins in the ten-race series. Finishing 2nd at Indy, from pole position, Peter returned to Grand Prix racing in a Tyrrell at the end of the year – signing-up with McLaren for a full season in 1972.

Peter Revson.

Proving as fast in practice as team-mate Hulme, the American put in a string of smooth, neat performances, scoring his first World Championship points for a 3rd place in South Africa. Surprising many by qualifying and finishing 3rd at Brands Hatch, Peter proved it was no fluke by qualifying 4th and finishing 3rd in Austria a month later. On the front row in both North American races, Peter

The 1973 British Grand Prix was the setting for a convincing win for Peter in a McLaren, having passed Peterson for the lead just after half distance.

scored a 2nd in Canada and drove an inspired race at Watkins Glen after an early pit stop only to retire when 6th.

Having scored a 2nd place in South Africa at the beginning of the 1973 season, Peter went on to a convincing first Grand Prix win at Silverstone, passing Peterson for the lead just after half-distance. A controversial win in the wet Canadian round as well as other minor placings pushed the American up to 5th place in the World Championship table at the end of the year.

Moving to the American-backed Shadow team in 1974, Peter immediately proved a front-runner in the two South American races but, during testing at Kyalami, South Africa, something snapped at the front end of his car sending it off the track into an Armco barrier where it burst into flames. The talented, versatile American, with the "playboy" image was beyond the help of his fellow drivers – a very sad loss to motor racing....

For The Record

First GP
1964 Belgium (Lotus 24-BRM)

GP Wins
1973 Britain (McLaren M23)
1973 Canada (McLaren M23)

Born on January 18, 1940, Pedro started his career on motorcycles – winning his native Mexican Motorcycle Championship at the age of 14! Moving on to cars in 1955, he raced Ferraris with his brother Ricardo in Mexico and South America before travelling to Europe to start his fourteen year, unbroken, association with the Le Mans 24-hour race.

Although distressed by Ricardo's fatal accident (while practising for the 1962 Mexican Grand Prix) Pedro continued his career – proving successful in Sports Cars with his Ferrari. In the 1963 United States Grand Prix, Pedro made his debut in a Lotus-BRM, but it was to be a year before he scored a point – in his home Mexican Grand Prix for 6th place in a Ferrari. Sinking into relative obscurity, Pedro nevertheless came home 4th in the 1965 International Trophy at Silverstone.

'On trial' for Cooper in 1967, Pedro hit the headlines by winning, albeit fortunately, the first race of the season in South Africa. Reliability led to points being scored in Monaco, France, Britain

Pedro Rodriguez.

and Mexico: enough for Pedro to be signed-up by BRM for 1968. With a competitive chassis, Pedro showed fine form in Belgium where he finished 2nd and in Holland and Canada where he was placed 3rd. However, his finest

Although leading here, Pedro – driving a BRM – eventually finished 2nd in the wet 1971 Dutch Grand Prix after an incredible dice with Ickx.

achievement of 1968 came when he won Le Mans with Branchi in a Ford – an achievement that foretold a great Sports Car career in the future.

A lean Grand Prix season in 1969 was followed by Pedro's best in 1970, for he was the sensation of Spa – making an excellent start to be placed 4th at the beginning of lap one. Rapidly, he hauled in, and overtook Rindt, Stewart and Amon to dominate and win the race. But for misfortune, Pedro could have added another two victories to his total in 1970, for in Italy he qualified 2nd and led briefly before retiring, and in the United States he looked a certain winner until he ran out of fuel! Undoubtedly, he was the Sports Car driver of the year in his Porsche, winning four races. Indeed, his total domination is summed-up by the fact that at Spa he was on pole and set a fastest lap of no less than 14 seconds better than the previous record!

In the 1971 Dutch Grand Prix he gave a magnificent demonstration of wet-weather driving, dicing with Ickx for the lead over the whole distance, eventually finishing 2nd. Once again in Sports Cars he was in devastating form, having already won four times in the year – but then, two weeks after winning at the Osterreichring in his Porsche 917, he was competing in an Interserie race at the Norisring when a tyre burst sending his car out of control and fatally injuring the Mexican.

Sports Car racing had been deprived of its leading exponent and most exciting driver. Pedro's career had been one of gradual improvement until he became one of the world's most disciplined and talented drivers. It was a tragedy that his life should be wasted when his career, at last, looked so promising.

For The Record

First GP
1963 United States (Lotus-BRM)

GP Wins
1967 South Africa (Cooper-Maserati)
1970 Belgium (BRM P153)

Swedish by birth, Finnish by nationality, Keijo 'Keke' Rosberg was born on December 6, 1948, the son of a vet. Like so many other drivers Keke began his career in karting, during 1965, and by the early 1970s he was a top name in European Formula Vee and Formula Super Vee.

Keke's fast and spectacular driving style took a while to develop, but soon American Fred Opert signed him up to drive in the 1976 European Formula 2 series. However, it took until 1977 before Keke made his mark, winning at Enna from pole position, finishing 2nd at Donington and 3rd at the Nurburgring to claim 6th place in the Championship. He also dominated the early part of the Canadian Formula Atlantic series picking up a 1st and two 2nds in the first four races.

Keke's Formula 1 debut came in 1978 when he raced the new Theodore in the South African Grand Prix. The car proved disappointing thereafter, failing to qualify again. Keke's great day came at the Silverstone International Trophy where he demonstrated his car control by pulling off a competent victory on the rain-soaked track. Switching to ATS mid-season, he proved that Silverstone was no fluke when he moved up to 4th place in the British Grand Prix before

Keke Rosberg.

retirement. Struggling for the rest of the season in various cars, Keke consoled himself with Formula 2, pulling off a convincing win at Donington, and finishing 2nd in the Formula Atlantic Championship.

At the start of 1979, Keke seemed to have been left out in the cold, and was without a Formula 1 drive, that is until Hunt retired mid-season allowing Keke to fill his place at the Wolf team. Failing to curb his ragged style, he nevertheless

Keke secured his first major Formula 1 drive when he replaced the retiring Hunt at Wolf midway through 1979.

had magnificent drives in Britain and especially Holland where he was running a steady 4th until retirement. Keke also proved to be the star of the Can-Am series in the fast, but fragile, Spyder.

With the Wolf-Fittipaldi merger, Keke remained to stay and drive alongside twice-World Champion Emerson Fittipaldi. Keke started the 1980 season with a smooth 3rd place behind Jones and Piquet in Argentina – a drive of surprising delicacy that confounded critics. Outqualifying Fittipaldi, he often put in superb practice times – in Germany and Canada especially – but, except for a 5th in Italy, retirements plagued the unfortunate Finn.

Great hopes were held for 1981 when Keke qualified 4th and finished 4th in the non-Championship South African Grand Prix at the beginning of the season, but soon the team's financial problems began to show, resulting in a series of non-qualifications and culminating in the team's withdrawing from the Austrian event.

His ability at last recognised, Keke has signed-up to drive for Williams in 1982 where he will surely prove to be a race winner.

For The Record

First GP
1978 South Africa (Theodore TR1)

Best GP Result
3rd 1980 Argentina (Fittipaldi F7)

The son of the President of the Chilean Federation of Motor Racing, Eliseo was born on November 14, 1954. His first taste of competition came when he co-drove in local rallies. He then took up racing a Mini Cooper, winning his national championship. Moving to Argentina to compete in their national championship, Eliseo's name sprang to prominence when he won the 1979 Argentine Grand Prix supporting Formula 2 event. This success allowed Eliseo to bring together enough money to race in the 1979 British Formula 3 Championship and eventually the 1980 Aurora Formula 1 series. Racing an ex-works Williams FW07, Eliseo won the Silverstone International Trophy, and both Thruxton races to finish 2nd behind team-mate de Villota in the Championship.

Arousing interest and sponsorship in Chile, Eliseo was able to move on to Grand Prix racing with the re-established March team in 1981. However, despite six attempts to qualify, Eliseo managed the feat only once, in San Marino. After Monaco, March decided to concentrate on a one-car team for Daly, so Eliseo was left without a drive until he joined Ensign.

Qualifying regularly, Eliseo had a series of excellent drives beginning in Germany where he set sixth fastest lap in the race. A good race in Austria was followed by an unexpected but well deserved World Championship point in Holland.

Eliseo Salazar.

Eliseo is no longer thought of as a useful Formula 1 driver merely because of his sponsorship; now it is his skill which is the first consideration. Indeed, he was hopeful of securing a Lotus drive in 1982 but instead will drive for ATS.

For The Record

First GP
1981 San Marino (March 811)

Best GP Result
6th 1981 Holland (Ensign N180B)

Although dumped by March halfway through the 1981 season, Eliseo proved his worth by putting together a string of competitive drives in the Ensign.

109

Born on January 29, 1950, the son of a car dealer, Jody raced both karts and bikes before competing in a self-modified Renault R8 in local saloon events during 1968. 1970 saw Formula Ford racing reach South Africa and, being the highest placed South African driver in the series, Jody won an air ticket to London and about £300 to start racing.

Proving to be the sensation of 1971, he recorded pole position and 2nd place in his first British Formula Ford race. Gaining the reputation of a fiery tearaway he quickly graduated to Formula 3 scoring several wins and coming 3rd in the Shell Super-Oil Championship. During the winter he returned home to race a Chevron B19 before signing a contract to race a Formula 2 McLaren.

Although Jody only scored one Formula 2 win during 1972, he beat many well-known drivers in other fine drives. McLaren were impressed enough to give him a race in an old McLaren at the United States Grand Prix and he ran 3rd for 15 laps ahead of Fittipaldi before spinning during a freak shower.

In a busy 1973 season Jody won the American Formula 5000 Championship and had some good placings in a

Jody Scheckter.

number of Can-Am races. His occasional Formula 1 drives showed flashes of inspiration, leading in South Africa and France, but Jody will best be remembered in 1973 for his spin on the second lap at Silverstone, starting a multiple accident which stopped the race.

After many years of trying, Jody curbed his aggressive driving style to secure three wins and the 1979 World Championship in a Ferrari.

1974 saw Jody's first regular Formula 1 drive, in a Tyrrell, nearly accomplishing the feat of scoring his first GP point and winning the World Championship in the same season (after victories in Sweden and Britain). 1975 gave Jody victory in his home South African Grand Prix. Then the arrival of the six-wheeled P34 Tyrrell, in 1976, won Jody the Swedish Grand Prix from the first pole position of his career, and a number of other good finishes put him 3rd in the Championship.

1977 showed that Jody was more than just a fast driver, he was a good test driver too, because he joined the new Wolf team and won first time out in Argentina. The team built a car for reliability rather than speed, and this paid off with more wins at Monaco and in Canada and six other top three finishes. Being runner-up in the World Championship was his reward and much was expected in 1978. However, the wing-car revolution started by Lotus meant that the Wolf immediately became outdated and a quickly built Wolf wing-car was not able to match the flying Lotus. Superb drives culminated in 2nd places in Germany and Canada however.

For 1979 Jody joined Ferrari aiming to win the World Championship – and he did! With only one retirement in the year, Jody's Ferrari proved both quick and reliable winning three races. Jody also proved that when necessary he could still produce a fighting drive, as was shown in Holland where, from 19th on the first lap, because of an overheated clutch on the startline, he climbed through the field to take 2nd place. It was, however, the mature and calculating Jody who took the title.

Jody seemed to lose his sparkle in 1980 and only once outqualified his team-mate Villeneuve in the uncompetitive Ferrari 312T5. He finished the season with only two points from a 5th place at Long Beach. Despite announcing his retirement before the end of the season, Jody had commitment enough to complete the season in a car that was definitely off the pace.

Jody was a deserving World Champion, the only surprise being that it took him so long to win the elusive title. He organised a series of World Cup motorcycle races in 1981, showing his continued interest in all forms of motorsport.

For The Record

First GP
1972 United States (McLaren M19A)

GP Wins
1974 Sweden (Tyrrell 007)
1974 Britain (Tyrrell 007)
1975 South Africa (Tyrrell 007)
1976 Sweden (Tyrrell P34)
1977 Argentina (Wolf WR1)
1977 Monaco (Wolf WR1)
1977 Canada (Wolf WR1)
1979 Belgium (Ferrari 312T4)
1979 Monaco (Ferrari 312T4)
1979 Italy (Ferrari 312T4)

World Champion
1979 (Ferrari)

This Australian driver was born on September 26, 1943. After successful races in both Formula 2 and hillclimbs, Tim arrived in England early in 1966 and raced in both saloon car and Formula 3 events. Unfortunately, in 1967, he was unable to afford a new Formula 3 car and so he updated an old Lotus. Still uncompetitive, his season was shortened by a suspension failure, and the inevitable shunt, at Crystal Palace.

With even less money in 1968, Tim was forced to compete in Formula Ford. He dominated the series and was offered a Formula 3 Chevron drive mid-season. 1969 saw Tim at the wheel of a works-assisted Formula 3 Brabham and, after some impressive drives, moved up to Formula 2 in 1970. Good drives at Pau and Rouen in his Brabham were followed by a superb 2nd place behind Regazzoni

Tim Schenken.

Tim on his way to a competitive 3rd in the 1971 Austrian event driving a Brabham.

at Paul Ricard – beating the likes of Cevert, Hill and Peterson. There followed Formula 1 drives in the de Tomaso, but an 11th in Canada was his best result.

In 1971 Tim was signed up by Brabham and in his first drive for them he came 4th in the Race of Champions at Brands Hatch. After a good drive in France, where he fought his way up to 5th before retirement, Tim scored his first World Championship point in Germany. Two weeks later he scored what was to be his best Grand Prix result, a 3rd in Austria, exactly a year after his Grand Prix debut. Three 2nds in Formula 2 put him 4th in the 1971 F2 Championship table.

Moving to Surtees in 1972, Tim celebrated by finishing 5th in his first Grand Prix with them, but was never to score again, despite encouraging grid positions in the mid-season races and a 3rd at the Oulton Park Gold Cup. The year was, however, a successful season in Ferrari Sports Cars for Tim, culminating with a win at the Nurburgring 1000km with Peterson.

Losing a regular Formula 1 drive in 1973, Tim had just one unsuccessful outing – in an Iso Marlboro in Canada. Formula 2 brought success in the form of three 3rds, a 2nd and a win at the Norisring in his Motul, following-up his success the year before at Hockenheim.

Tim made a brief return to Formula 1 in 1974 in the Trojan team and was even given a drive in a Lotus 76 in the States but failed to qualify. After a fruitful 1975 season in Interserie and Group 4, Tim joined forces with Howden Ganley to build a Formula Ford car for 1976. The company is still thriving. Since then Tim has raced with varying degrees of success in Sports and Touring Cars, winning the 1977 Nurburgring 1000Km in a Porsche Turbo.

After his victorious seasons in Formula Ford and Formula 3 many saw him as a Grand Prix winner of the future. But unfortunately Tim never managed to prove his ability and soon lost a regular Formula 1 drive despite good Sports Car results.

For The Record

First GP
1970 Austria (de Tomaso 505)

Best GP Result
3rd 1971 Austria (Brabham B 33)

This determined German-speaking Swiss was born in Fribourg on July 7, 1936. Everything he achieved in life was the result of his own hard work and competitive abilities, for he came from a poor home background and had the additional disadvantage of a malformed right foot. Starting his career on two wheels he won the Swiss Motorcycle Championship in 1959 before turning to four wheels, acquiring a Fiat-Strangvellini for 1960 hillclimbs. Joining Scuderia Filipinetti he raced a Lotus 18 and later a Lotus 20 during the 1961 season, becoming European Formula Junior Champion and winner of the Junior World Trophy.

Moving on to Formula 1 in 1962 he came 6th in the non-Championship Brussels Grand Prix before making his debut World Championship drive at Spa in a Lotus 24. After scoring his first World Championship point in the French Grand Prix he was voted the Wolfgang von Trips Memorial Trophy for independent drivers. Encouraging performances in a Brabham in 1964 led to Rob Walker's signing up Jo for his team. At Goodwood Jo crashed, breaking a leg, but in just six weeks – still in great pain – he finished 6th at the tough Monaco circuit.

1966 showed that Jo's maxim for the future was to run in as many races as possible – Formula 1, Formula 2, Sports Cars and Hillclimbs. However, his F1 Cooper-Maserati was unreliable and his

Joseph Siffert.

only real success was winning the Index of Performance at Le Mans for two consecutive years – 1966 and 1967. Tremendous success in Sports Cars in 1968 was followed by a 2nd at the Monaco Grand Prix before everything went right for Jo's first win, in Britain. This was followed by good performances at the Canadian and Mexican GPs.

1969 saw the start of Jo's great Sports Car partnership with Brian Redman – winning five races that year for Porsche. Formula 1 was not so

Jo scored a dominant win in 1971 driving a BRM at the ultra-fast Osterreichring.

successful however, but he did come 4th in the Can-Am Championship. Despite Sports Car success and a Formula 2 win at Rouen, 1970 saw Jo's worst Formula 1 season when, in a March, he failed to score a single point.

1971 was different, for he joined BRM and was always high on the grid and the lap charts. It is possibly Jo's performance at the Osterreichring that will always be remembered: from pole position he led from start to finish, setting fastest lap on the way. This pushed him up to 4th in the World Championship – making 1971 his best ever year as he also won the Sports Car Championship for Porsche.

However, on October 24, 1971, at the Brands Hatch race in honour of the new World Champion Jackie Stewart, Jo was on pole again but made a bad start. He began a typically fighting drive through the field, but it was a drive doomed to end in tragedy. A tyre deflated, sending Jo's car spinning out of control to explode on impact with a bank. Joseph Siffert, the master of endurance racing, died almost instantly, asphyxiated without pain.

For The Record

First GP
1962 Belgium (Lotus 24 Climax)

GP Wins
1968 Britain (Lotus-Ford)
1971 Austria (BRM P160)

John Young 'Jackie' Stewart was born in Dumbarton, Scotland on June 11, 1939, the younger son of a Jaguar car dealer. Originally his first love was trap-shooting – reaching near-Olympic standards – but as his interest in shooting waned, so his interest in motor racing increased. His elder brother, Jimmy, had competed internationally but an accident had led his parents to disapprove of motor-racing. However, despite parental opposition, Jackie's mind was decided following a test session at Oulton Park in 1962 – he had to tackle motor-racing seriously!

After two years of club racing, Jackie's naturally smooth, yet aggressive driving style became apparent and so Ken Tyrrell signed the promising newcomer to drive his Formula 3 Coopers in 1964. Jackie's career never looked back, for that year he won all but two of the Formula 3 races he entered as well as gaining Formula 2 experience.

Although tempted by Lotus, Jackie shrewdly decided to move into Grand Prix racing with BRM in 1965. Scoring a point on his debut in South Africa, this incredible young man managed to lead at Monaco – only his second start(!) – but finished 3rd after an uncharacteristic spin. Immediately proving to be a worthy rival to Jim Clark, Jackie's first Grand Prix win came in Italy where he fought and won a close duel with his team leader, Hill.

Jackie Stewart.

Much was expected of 1966, and Jackie obliged by winning the first round in Monaco. At Spa his career seemed to suffer a setback, for he hit a freak shower during the race and spun off – coming to a halt semi-conscious in a petrol-soaked car. Although rescued by Hill, he suffered a broken shoulder, a cracked rib and fuel burns which ever after made Jackie very safety conscious – eventually using his influence to improve the safety of many of the world's circuits.

It was not until joining Ken Tyrrell's Matra outfit in 1968 that Jackie began

Having secured his third World Title two weeks earlier in Italy, Jackie finished 5th in his final Grand Prix – the wet 1973 Canadian event, driving a Tyrrell.

winning again, but his Championship hopes suffered an early dive when he broke his wrist in an early season Formula 2 race. Nevertheless, three superb wins followed in Holland (where he still had to wear a support for his arm), Germany (where he won by an incredible four-minute margin) and the United States.

In 1969 he dominated the season, using his accurate and polished driving style to win six races to take the Championship. However, his defence of the title in 1970 never really lifted off the ground for his early season speed was never matched, and his car proved unreliable. It was not until Tyrrell produced his own cars in the end-of-season American races that Jackie dominated again, giving a warning of what was to come in 1971. Jackie was on top of the rostrum no less than six times during the 1971 eleven-race series.

World Champion for a second time, Jackie's 1972 season – following his dominant win in Argentina – was plagued by mechanical and medical problems and, although he surfaced briefly from the doldrums to win in France, it was not until the Canadian and American races that he showed true form again to finish runner-up in the World Championship.

Having already decided that 1973 would be his last Grand Prix season before retirement, Jackie wanted to end his scintillating career on a high note. Victories in South Africa, Belgium, Monaco and Holland took Jackie beyond both Fangio's and Clark's amazing records of Grand Prix wins; and his final win in Germany – an impressive display of complete domination – took his tally to an incredible 27 and helped him to his **third** World Championship!

Jackie has still not completely retired for he remains the sponsors' delight by participating in television commentaries and promotional work. So much is he respected that, in the winter of 1981, he was offered approximately £3 million to return to Formula 1! Although refusing the offer, Jackie can still rightly claim to be **The Driver** of his era because he completely dominated the Grand Prix scene between 1969 and 1973.

For The Record

First GP
1965 South Africa (BRM)

GP Wins
1965 Italy (BRM)
1966 Monaco (BRM)
1968 Holland (Matra MS10)
1968 Germany (Matra MS10)
1968 United States (Matra MS10)
1969 South Africa (Matra MS10)
1969 Spain (Matra MS80)
1969 Holland (Matra MS80)
1969 France (Matra MS80)
1969 Britain (Matra MS80)
1969 Italy (Matra MS80)
1970 Spain (March 701)
1971 Spain (Tyrrell 003)
1971 Monaco (Tyrrell 003)
1971 France (Tyrrell 003)
1971 Britain (Tyrrell 003)
1971 Germany (Tyrrell 003)
1971 Canada (Tyrrell 003)
1972 Argentina (Tyrrell 003)
1972 France (Tyrrell 003)
1972 Canada (Tyrrell 005)
1972 United States (Tyrrell 005)
1973 South Africa (Tyrrell 006)
1973 Belgium (Tyrrell 006)
1973 Monaco (Tyrrell 006)
1973 Holland (Tyrrell 006)
1973 Germany (Tyrrell 006)

World Champion
1969 (Matra)
1971 (Tyrrell)
1973 (Tyrrell)

Born on July 11, 1943, this likeable, bespectacled German began his four-wheel career racing Porsches in 1964. Hitting the limelight by winning the 1967 Targo Florio with Paul Hawkins, Rolf went on to victories at Daytona and Montlhery in 1968 with a Porsche. His first single-seater drive came in the Formula 2 division of the 1969 German Grand Prix, where he finished 4th in a Lotus. This, combined with further successful Sports Car races led to a regular drive with Brabham in 1970.

Making his Grand Prix debut in South Africa, he scored his first points in Holland for a 5th place. In Austria, however, he drove a copybook race from low down on the grid to finish 3rd. Following a 1971 season spent with Surtees, the highlights of which came when he was lying 2nd in the non-Championship Argentine GP before being punted off by eventual winner Amon, Rolf's Grand Prix career took a dive in 1972 when he drove the uncompetitive Eifelland.

Although disappointing during his occasional Grand Prix drives with

Rolf Stommelen.

Brabham in 1973 and with Lola in 1974, Rolf proved his worth in Alfa Romeo Sports Cars. In a F1 Hill GH, Rolf was in 3rd place soon after the start of the 1975 Spanish Grand Prix and took over the lead when Andretti spun. For five

For five incredible laps, Rolf led the 1975 Spanish Grand Prix until the rear wing flew off his Hill, resulting in a horrifying accident.

incredible laps he led, but suddenly his rear wing flew off sending him into a horrifying accident which resulted in the race being stopped. After a long convalescence Rolf thankfully returned to the cockpit at the end of the year.

Rejoining Porsche Sports Cars in 1976, he won at Enna, as well as at the WCM Watkins Glen round. As a bonus in 1976 he had a couple of races in a Brabham finishing 6th in Germany – and one unsuccessful outing in a Hesketh. After wins at Mugello and at the Nurburgring in a Porsche 935, Rolf raised enough sponsorship to join the newly-formed Arrows Grand Prix team in 1978, but had a poor season. Reverting to Sports Cars in 1979, he was closing fast on the leader at Le Mans at the finish but had to be content with a 2nd, although winning the IMSA class. Further victories followed and in 1981 he scored a hat-trick of wins in the IMSA series.

A top Sports Car exponent, chiefly with Porsche, Rolf's occasional Grand Prix drives have always been fairly impressive.

For The Record

First GP
1970 South Africa (Brabham BT33)

Best GP Result
3rd 1970 Austria (Brabham BT33)

This tall German was born on January 1, 1951, the son of a famous prewar Auto Union Grand Prix driver, the late Hans Stuck. Often spectacular, and excelling in atrocious weather conditions, Hans began his career at the tender age of nine by driving karts and a miniature 600cc BMW-engined car. At 13 he was lapping the Nurburgring at competitive speeds and by the time he was 17 he began to race seriously, chiefly for BMW in saloon events.

Moving through Formula 3 in 1972, Hans competed with some success in Formula 2 the following year. Encouraged by BMW, March took Hans on in 1974 to race both Formula 1 and Formula 2. In the latter he scored three fine wins to finish second in the European Championship, and in Formula 1 he gave a dashing performance in South Africa to finish 5th. In the next Grand Prix, in Spain, he finished 4th in the wet. After a disappointing remainder to the 1974 season, he was rested for the first part of 1975, but kept his hand in by racing BMWs in America. But, despite qualifying 4th in Austria, he failed to figure prominently on his return to

Hans-Joachim Stuck.

Formula 1, although he finished 2nd in the Hockenheim Formula 2 race.

Another season of ill-luck and unreliability followed in 1976 with March. Hans' big break came when he signed-up for Brabham soon after the start of the 1977 season, following Pace's flying

Hans' moment of glory came in 1977 at Watkins Glen where, in atrocious weather conditions, he led for fourteen laps until he spun off when his Brabham jumped out of gear.

accident. Although lucky to finish 6th in Spain, he had a great drive at Monaco – holding off a determined Lauda until retiring. Inspired in front of his home crowd, Hans scored a well-deserved 3rd place in Germany and followed it up with another excellent 3rd in Austria. Hans' moment of glory came, however, at Watkins Glen, for, having qualified on the front row of the grid he drove brilliantly, leading a Grand Prix for the first time in his career only to spin off when his car jumped out of gear after 14 rain-drenched laps.

With Shadow in 1978, Hans' only result of merit was 5th in Britain – astonishing, considering he was 25th on the first lap! Joining ATS, Hans only figured strongly at Watkins Glen where he finished 5th. Since then Hans has not secured a Grand Prix drive and so his exploits have been confined to Sports Cars, winning the shortened 1981 Nurburgring 1000Km in a BMW M1 with Nelson Piquet. Although inconsistent, Hans has the talent to turn on the speed when the mood takes him.

For The Record

First GP
1974 Argentina (March 741)

Best GP Result
3rd 1977 Germany (Brabham BT45B)
3rd 1977 Austria (Brabham BT45B)

This good looking quietly spoken, blond Swiss was born on September 18, 1951. Before conscription intervened in 1971, Marc had planned to become a designer, but instead he became a tank driver before occasionally racing karts. In 1972 he won the Swiss Class B Karting Championship, and the following year he became a member of the National Kart team, finishing 3rd in the European Championship. A course at the Jim Russell School, based at the Osterreichring, during Autumn 1973 attracted the attention of sponsors who helped him to compete in the 1974 German Formula Vee Championship, in which he finished runner-up.

Marc Surer.

Plans for a full season in Formula 3 during 1975 fell through and so it was not until 1976 that he made real progress into this Formula. Racing a March, and later a Chevron, Marc finished 2nd in the German Championship and 4th in the European Championship – including a fine 2nd place at Zandvoort behind Patrese. A member of the BMW Junior team, he notched-up some useful results during 1977 in the German Group 5 Championship and shot to prominence when he qualified a superb 2nd, and finished 4th, at the end-of-season Donington Formula 2 round.

Capably backing-up Giacomelli in the 1978 European Formula 2 Championship, with no less than six 2nd places, Marc was placed runner-up in the series. In 1979 he scored two well-deserved victories at the Nurburgring and Vallelunga early in the season; eventually snatching the title by two points from Henton by finishing 2nd in the final round at Donington. As European Formula 2 Champion, Marc was given the opportunity to drive the Ensign Grand Prix car at the end of the season, and, after failing to qualify at both Monza and Montreal, finally made

Marc was the revelation of the 1981 Brazilian Grand Prix, for he finished an amazing 4th having set fastest lap on the rain-soaked track in his under-financed Ensign.

the grid at Watkins Glen only to retire during the race.

Signing for ATS in 1980, Marc went well initially – especially in Brazil where he was placed an impressive 7th – but after a serious accident in South Africa he slid down the grids as the team floundered.

Returning to Ensign in 1981, he immediately showed his ability by running 6th in the non-Championship South African Grand Prix before retirement. In Brazil, though, he was the star of the race, setting fastest lap and finishing a brilliant 4th on the rain-soaked track. Further consistent drives followed in Monaco, Britain and Holland to show that Marc is a potential Grand Prix winner given the right equipment. That equipment may well be given to him now that he has signed up to lead the Arrows team in 1982, even though his season suffered a setback when he broke a leg testing in preparation for the South African Grand Prix in January.

For The Record

First GP
1979 United States, East (Ensign N179)

Best GP Result
4th 1981 Brazil (Ensign N180B)

Versatile, conscientious and hard-working, 'Big John' Surtees was born on February 11, 1934, the son of a garage owner and enthusiastic motorcyclist. Hugely successful on motorcycles – winning the World Championship in 1956, 1958 and 1959 – John tested for both Aston Martin and Vanwall cars in 1959 but began his career on four wheels in his own private Formula 2 Cooper in 1959. He also signed a contract to race Formula Junior Coopers for Ken Tyrrell.

In 1960, John was offered a Formula 1 Lotus drive when his motorcycle commitments allowed. In Britain he finished 2nd and impressed by qualifying on pole and leading comfortably until retirement in Portugal. After winning another two motorcycle Championships in the same year, he finally quit two-wheels for four, to race a Cooper with little success in 1961.

Good mid-season form, including 2nds in Britain and Germany in 1962, earned John 4th place in the Championship. His move to Ferrari, in 1963, immediately showed his potential – at Monaco he was up to 2nd, setting fastest lap, before being forced to drop back to finish 4th. In Holland he came 3rd, in Britain 2nd, and in Germany, from 2nd on the grid, 'Big John' won his first Grand Prix, setting fastest lap on the way.

John Surtees.

1964 was the year when John Surtees made history, as he became the first driver to win a World Championship on both **two** and **four** wheels. It was not an easy success, however. Two victories (Germany and Italy) and a series of high placings gave 'Big John' a chance of taking the F1 title in Mexico – the last round of the season. Both Graham Hill and Jim Clark retired, so team-mate Bandini allowed John through into 2nd place allowing him to take the World Championship.

John's successful career came to an end after a one-off race in the 1972 Italian Grand Prix where he race-tested the then new TS14 model.

A 2nd in the South African Grand Prix proved to be John's best result of the 1965 season, a year that ended dramatically with a crash in a Can-Am car. A crash that many thought would end his career; however, doctors had reckoned without Surtees' determination!

Despite victory in Belgium, a disagreement with Ferrari at Le Mans in 1966 led to a split: John driving a Cooper-Maserati for the rest of the season and winning in Mexico to come 2nd in the Championship. Consolation came in the Can-Am series which he won in a Lola.

Joining Honda in 1967, John commenced the tremendous task of helping the team to success by winning in Italy. A disappointing 1968 season with Honda prompted John to join BRM in 1969, picking up a 3rd in the United States. By this time John had formed his own company and had introduced his new Surtees TS5 Formula 5000 car, which won five races in 1969.

John had to bide his time in a McLaren until his own TS7 was ready mid-season. He unveiled his new car a few days before the 1970 British Grand Prix and it had a fine debut until engine problems let him down. Everything clicked at the Oulton Park Gold Cup where John was easily fastest in practice, won the first half of the race and stayed close enough to Rindt in the second half to claim overall victory.

With a TS9 in 1971 John gradually moved up the grid as the season progressed and was rewarded by a 5th in the wet Dutch race, a 6th at Silverstone and another win in the Oulton Park Gold Cup.

John only made one more race appearance, in the 1972 Italian Grand Prix to race-test the new TS14, before retiring to direct his own team. However, a combination of ill-fortune and lack of finance forced the team to leave the World Championship scene at the end of 1978. 'Big John' now runs a Honda dealership in Kent.

For The Record

First GP
1960 Monaco (Lotus Climax)

GP Wins
1963 Germany (Ferrari 625)
1964 Germany (Ferrari 625)
1964 Italy (Ferrari (625)
1966 Belgium (Ferrari (312)
1966 Mexico (Cooper-Maserati)
1967 Italy (Honda)

World Champion
1964 (Ferrari)

Born in Paris on June 25, 1949, Patrick, forsaking a successful skiing career, started motor-racing in 1971 at Paul Ricard's Renault-Elf racing drivers' school. His 1st place in the Pilote Elf final won him a scholarship and a Formula Renault drive for the 1972 season. He finished runner-up to Arnoux, despite scoring six victories and setting eight lap records!

Moving on to Formula 2 in 1974, Patrick won the non-Championship race at Nogaro late in the year after a promising season and earned himself a works March drive in 1975. He notched up three pole positions, yet only won at Nogaro and so had to be content with equal 2nd in the Championship. Once again, in 1976, Patrick won at Nogaro but this time had to be content with 3rd place in the series.

Patrick Tambay.

As James Hunt's team-mate in 1978, Patrick proved successful in the McLaren M26, finishing in the points on five occasions.

In 1977 Patrick had his first taste of Formula 1, in a Surtees which he failed to qualify in France. Later, he made an impressive Grand Prix debut in Britain driving an Ensign. After another excellent run in Austria, Patrick held a fine 3rd for many laps in Holland before retiring on the last lap, out of fuel. However, he was still credited with 5th place, a result he repeated in Canada.

These late season performances were enough to urge McLaren to sign-up the likeable Frenchman to partner James Hunt in 1978; Patrick impressing by finishing 6th, first time out, in Argentina. Although gradually slipping down the grid Patrick showed much brio and determination to finish 4th in Sweden, 5th in Italy, and 6th in Britain and the States.

1979 was a frustrating year for Patrick in which he scored no World Championship points, although his driving was not as bad as the lack of results would seem to indicate: many good late season drives being spoilt by engine problems. Nevertheless Patrick lost his McLaren drive and so had to compete in the Can-Am championship in 1980. He won six of the ten races to clinch the title he had previously won in 1977.

Returning to the fray is difficult, indeed rare, in Formula 1 and so it surprised many when Patrick gambled on joining the Theodore team in 1981. The first-time-out 6th place at Long Beach, proved to be Patrick's best result of the year – despite joining the Ligier team mid-season as a replacement for Jabouille. Flashes of inspiration were evident in Italy, where he was challenging for 3rd before retirement, and Las Vegas, where he outqualified Laffite in both timed practices having learnt that he had lost his drive with the team.

For 1982 Patrick was to have driven an Arrows car for the first few races of the season following Surer's unfortunate accident, but, frustrated by the political squabbling at the South African Grand Prix, he reluctantly announced his retirement from Formula 1 in favour of furthering his already successful career in America.

For The Record

First GP
1977 Britain (Ensign N177)

Best GP Result
4th 1978 Sweden (McLaren M26)

Gilles Villeneuve, a driver of great determination who maintained a sense of fun, was born on January 18, 1952. The French-Canadian's interest in cars and engines began at his father's Honda garage and developed when he began racing snowmobiles at the age of 13. This culminated in his winning the Canadian Championship in 1973, and the World Title the next year. With his winnings Gilles took up first Formula Ford and then Formula Atlantic, finishing 5th in the 1975 series. Proving the sensation of the 1976 season, Gilles carried off both American and Canadian Formula Atlantic titles, beating Formula 1 stars Jones, Hunt and Brambilla at the Trois Rivieres round.

With the 1977 Canadian title under his belt, tales of an incredibly quick driver with remarkable reflexes, great courage and a spectacular style filtered through to the ears of Formula 1 teams. A sensational debut with an outdated McLaren at the 1977 British Grand Prix led to Ferrari signing him up to partner Reutemann when Lauda defected to Brabham, before the season was out. In his first race in a Ferrari Gilles spun out, and in Japan he ran over the back wheel of Peterson's Tyrrell, launching the Ferrari into a prohibited area, and sadly killing two spectators leading many to question the contract Ferrari had made with Gilles for 1978.

Gilles' natural talent first came to the fore when he led from the start at Long Beach in 1978, giving an impressive 39-lap demonstration of verve and car control until crashing when overtaking a back-marker. In Belgium, Gilles was the only driver able to threaten Andretti's lead before tyre failure dropped him to 4th, thus scoring his first World Championship points. Learning by his mistakes, Gilles made impressive progress from mid-season – then, in front of his home crowd at Montreal, in the year's last Grand Prix, Gilles got everything right to score the first brilliant Grand Prix victory of his career.

1979 saw the youthful exuberance of Gilles turn him into one of the pacemakers in Grand Prix racing. Three

Gilles Villeneuve.

impressive victories represented just the tip of the iceberg of the Canadian's talent. Who can forget his drive through the field in Belgium, or his wheel-to-wheel tussle with Arnoux in France, let alone his amazing start in Austria – taking the lead by the first corner from the third row of the grid? His never-say-die attitude in bringing his stricken, three-wheeled Ferrari back to his pit in Holland showed his will to win, a will that brought him 2nd place in the Championship.

1980 proved to be a disaster for Ferrari, Gilles' talent being rewarded only by a couple of 5ths and a couple of 6ths – so it was with much anticipation that the arrival of the new Ferrari Turbo in 1981 was heralded. Soon proving both reliable and fast, Gilles led in San Marino for a time from pole position before scoring two faultless victories on the trot in Monaco and Spain. The team seemed to lose direction after that, a 3rd in Canada being a credit to Gilles' amazing car control on the wet track.

With the arrival of the fantastic 126C2 in 1982, Gilles broke the Fiorano test track record on his first outing in the car by an amazing 1.5 seconds emphasising his ability and the very real potential he had for becoming a future World Champion.

Tragically, Gilles lost his life after being thrown from his car in an accident during practice for the 1982 Belgian Grand Prix.

Masterful car control combined with the powerful Ferrari turbo engine allowed Gilles to score two fine wins in 1981 – the first of which came here, at Monaco.

For The Record

First GP
1977 Britain (McLaren M23)

GP Wins
1978 Canada (Ferrari 213T3)

1979 South Africa (Ferrari 312T4)
1979 United States, West (Ferrari 312T4)
1979 United States, East (Ferrari 213T4)
1981 Monaco (Ferrari 126C)
1981 Spain (Ferrari 126C)

John was born in Belfast on May 4, 1946, the son of a garage owner. In 1964 John began racing saloons; by 1967 he was driving a Brabham in Irish Formule Libre events. An impressive number of wins in Ireland, and occasionally in Britain, led to a Formula 2 drive at Thruxton in 1969. On sensational form, John was 5th in an outdated Lotus before crashing. He completed the 1969 season in Irish Formule Libre.

In 1970 his Formula 2 season was cut short by a huge crash at Rouen due to a puncture, resulting in a broken arm and leg. By the end of 1971 he was again proving to be one of the most consistently fast men in the Formula. Despite his speed and talent, results failed to come John's way, but even so he had a couple of Formula 1 drives for

John Watson.

During a classic duel, John (No. 28) momentarily surges into the lead of the 1976 Dutch Grand Prix. Although persistently pressurising the eventual winner, James Hunt (No. 11), his Penske retired at two-thirds distance with gearbox failure.

the Brabham team in 1973. Competing in a full Grand Prix season with a privately-entered Brabham in 1974, John scored his first point at Monaco after a splendid struggle with Fittipaldi, the season ending on a high note with a 4th in Austria despite a pit stop, and a 5th in the States.

After a disappointing 1975 season with Surtees, John replaced the late Mark Donohue as team leader of Penske in 1976 and soon bounced back on form with a 5th in South Africa. The arrival of a new car mid-season allowed him to score 3rd places in France and Britain. It was in Austria though that John made his mark. From 2nd on the grid he won the race fair and square on pure speed, but by doing so he had to shave off his beard to honour a promise made to team owner Roger Penske! In Holland the Ulsterman hounded, first Peterson, and then Hunt, for the lead, trying everything to pass, until his gearbox broke. A front-runner for the rest of the season, John was beached when Penske abandoned their Formula 1 project but was soon signed up by Brabham for 1977.

At the end of 1977 he had a mere nine points in the World Championship but this does not reveal the countless races John should, and could, have won ... In Argentina he led until his tyres went off; at Monaco having set pole, he was 2nd when he spun out; in Belgium he led from the line only to be punted off by Andretti; in Sweden he led but eventually had to retire; in France he ran out of fuel on the last lap when leading comfortably; in Britain he was holding off Hunt's challenge until retiring from the lead; and in Germany he was just about to take 1st place from Scheckter when his engine blew!

Again in 1978 John was out of luck at Monaco when he led for half the race until brake failure twice caught him out, and in France he was the only person to lead race winner Andretti. However, many finishes in the top six, including an inherited 2nd, in Italy, meant that John finished 6th in the Championship.

The Irishman's fortunes as McLaren Team Leader in 1979 and 1980 looked good, for in his first race for the team he finished 3rd in Argentina. Uncompetitive machinery, however, pushed John "Watswrong" (as his team christened him) off the rostrum and his morale hit an alltime low when he failed to qualify at Monaco in 1980, but excellent late-season drives – especially in Canada – confirmed his ability and experience.

A 3rd during 1981 in Spain and a 2nd in France led many to joke that John would win the next race in Britain, and so end the long drought. He did: overtaking Arnoux's ailing Renault a handful of laps from the finish! The season ended with a fine 2nd, in the wet, in Canada, boding well for a good 1982 season with Lauda as team-mate.

Undoubtedly one of Formula 1's best drivers, John has so often been frustrated by sheer bad luck.

For The Record

First GP
1973 Britain (Brabham BT37)

GP Wins
1976 Austria (Penske PC4)
1981 Britain (McLaren MP4)

Born September 30, 1941, this volatile Swedish driver started racing with a Mini-Cooper in the 1960s, but found that he could only manage five or six events in a year. In 1967 he progressed to driving a Formula 3 Brabham BT18, and proved successful with nine victories in Scandinavia on his way to winning the Swedish Championship. In 1968 and 1969 he proved to be one of the fastest Formula 3 drivers in Europe, along with Ronnie Peterson and Tim Schenken. For the 1968 season he bought a Tecno and won eleven Internationals before becoming a works Chevron driver in 1969.

These years in Formula 3 earned Reine the reputation of being a smooth, stylish driver as well as a clever tactician, in Formula 3 terms. Some people, however, suggest that Reine was never as quick after being beaten by Ronnie Peterson in the Monaco 1969 Formula 3 event. Nevertheless Reine won six races in the works Chevron B15, including the difficult Pau race and a dead heat with Tim Schenken at Montlhery. Reine even tried his hand at Le Mans in the thundering 7-litre Filipinetti Corvette as well as having some outings in Lola GT cars.

Reine Wisell.

These successes led to a drive in the 1970 International Trophy meeting where he came 5th in a McLaren M7A. Things happened fast towards the end of the year as Reine scored three wins on

Reine at the 1971 British Grand Prix struggling with the Lotus Turbine, the heat-haze from which may be seen at the rear of the car.

the trot in a Formula 5000 McLaren-Chevrolet M10B, and was offered a drive for Lotus in the remaining World Championship rounds. In the States Reine made an excellent debut in the Lotus 72, qualifying 9th and finishing 3rd, but success eluded him after that. Struggling with the Lotus Turbine car for part of the 1971 season, Reine managed to salvage nine points with the Lotus 72 to place himself 9th in the World Championship after seven finishes in the eleven-race series, as well as winning the Pau Formula 2 race in a Lotus 69.

This reliability ended when Reine moved to the five-car BRM team as a stand-in for Beltoise at the 1972 Argentine Grand Prix. Reine competed in five out of the first ten races of the season, his best result being 12th, before rejoining Lotus as a replacement for Dave Walker at the end of that year. Without a 1973 Formula 1 drive Reine returned to endurance racing where he had come 6th in a Lola at the Sebring 12-hours the previous year. To this Reine added a 6th at the Dijon 1000Km and a win in the Nurburgring Formula 2 race.

His final Formula 1 drive came in the 1974 Swedish Grand Prix when he replaced Stuck in a March, but despite qualifying quite well he retired. Since then he has competed in the World Championship of Makes and the European Car Championship with only moderate success, chiefly with Porsche, Chevrolet and BMW. Seriously considering retirement, he only competed in a very limited number of races during 1981 – including the Spa 24-hours – as he found travelling to and from his home in Sri Lanka rather trying!

It would have been interesting to see the talent of this superb Formula 3 driver developed further in Formula 1 as, given the right car and more experience, Reine would surely have delivered the goods.

For The Record

First GP
1970 United States (Lotus 72)

Best GP Result
3rd 1970 United States (Lotus 72)

This Italian driver was born in Turin on December 12, 1946. A former Pirelli tyre-testing engineer, he began his racing career in 1971 in Formula Fiat. His early career was confined to Italy, but in 1973 he won the Italian Formula Ford Championship and in 1975 he hit the limelight when he had a fortunate victory in the prestigious Monaco Formula 3 race.

As a result, he was offered a Formula 1 drive at the Italian Grand Prix in a Williams. A mere three-quarters of a second behind team leader Laffite in practice, he seemed to accustom himself well to the power of the car but only managed to finish a steady 14th.

A further Grand Prix drive in Brazil during 1976 followed, again for Williams, and this time Renzo impressed by qualifying ahead of his team-mate Ickx and by leading him for most of the race. However, after that one-off drive he returned to Formula 3.

Backed by Italian industrialist Franco Ambrosio, Renzo joined the Shadow team at the beginning of 1977. With an outdated car, he proved to be a regular qualifier and in Brazil he surprised many when he drove a sensible, if cautious, race to finish 6th in a Grand Prix in which only seven crossed the line. Unfortunately for Renzo he lost his Shadow drive after the Spanish race following a disagreement with Ambrosio, but, undeterred, Renzo continued racing occasionally, scoring a 5th place at Imola in a Chevron Sports car.

Renzo Zorzi.

It can be said that Renzo made the most of the opportunities presented to him and although not a top-line Formula 1 driver, he has earned himself a place in the record books for his efforts.

For The Record

First GP
1975 Italy (Williams FW02)

Best GP Result
6th 1977 Brazil (Shadow DN5)

Renzo finished an encouraging 6th in the 1977 Brazilian Grand Prix having driven a steady race in his Shadow.

Andrea de Adamich

Chris Amon

Mario Andretti

Elio de Angelis

Rene Arnoux

Jean-Pierre Beltoise

Slim Borgudd

Vittorio Brambilla

Tony Brise

Andrea de Cesaris

Francois Cevert

Eddie Cheever

Derek Daly

Patrick Depailler

Mark Donohue

Emerson Fittipaldi

Wilson Fittipaldi

George Follmer

Howden Ganley

Peter Gethin

Bruno Giacomelli

Mike Hailwood

Graham Hill

Denny Hulme

James Hunt

Jacky Ickx

Jean-Pierre Jabouille

Jean-Pierre Jarier

Alan Jones

Jacques Laffite

Niki Lauda (pre 1982)

Niki Lauda (1982)

Gijs van Lennep

Lella Lombardi

Nigel Mansell

Jochen Mass

Arturio Merzario

Gunnar Nilsson

Jackie Oliver

Carlos Pace

Riccardo Patrese

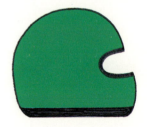

Henri Pescarolo

Ronnie Peterson

Nelson Piquet

Didier Pironi

Alain Prost

Tom Pryce

Hector Rebaque

Brian Redman

Clay Regazzoni

Carlos Reutemann

Peter Revson

Pedro Rodriguez

Keke Rosberg

Eliseo Salazar

Jody Scheckter

Tim Schenken

Joseph Siffert

Jackie Stewart

Rolf Stommelen

Hans Stuck

Marc Surer

John Surtees

Patrick Tambay

Gilles Villeneuve

John Watson

Reine Wisell

Renzo Zorzi